This Ain't Hell...
But You Can See It From Here!

A Gulf War Sketchbook
by Barry McWilliams

Edited by Colin Sorel McWilliams

PRESIDIO

THIS AIN'T HELL...BUT YOU CAN SEE IT FROM HERE!
A Gulf War Sketchbook by Barry McWilliams

Published by Presidio Press
505B San Marin Drive, Suite 300, Novato, California 94945

Library of Congress Cataloging in Publication Data

McWilliams, Barry 1942—
  This ain't hell—but you can see it from here! : a Gulf War sketchbook /
  by Barry McWilliams ; edited by Colin Sorel McWilliams. — 1st ed.

   ISBN 0-89141-443-6

   1. Persian Gulf War, 1991—United States—Anecdotes.
   I. McWilliams, Barry.   II. Title
DS79.72.M39   1992
956.704'3—dc20
                                                          91-36322
                                                          CIP

Printed in the United States of America

This book is dedicated to the memory of Commander John "Bug" Roach, United States Navy, lost on October 9, 1991, while flying a training mission over Southern California.

A Vietnam vet who had logged almost 1,000 carrier landings, many of them in the Persian Gulf, Bug was a legend in his own time. He represented the finest attributes of a military professional. He was brave, dedicated, and caring—an inspiration to all who knew him, and a very funny guy.

Contents

The Storm
THE GROUND WAR

The Shaft

Foreword

In January 1991, just after the Air War against Saddam began, I called my artist buddy, Glenn Eure, at his gallery in Nags Head, North Carolina.

"Glenn, I'm going to try to make it over to Saudi Arabia and draw some cartoons," I said.

"You won't believe this," said Glenn, "but I've been trying for weeks to get there myself." Then he told me how he'd called the Army a number of times offering to "re-up." Glenn was a 23-year Army veteran, most of it spent with the 82nd Airborne Division, but they had repeatedly turned him down.

"We're *not* accepting any *pot-bellied* battle veterans at this time," a female recruiter in Maryland had told him.

"Well, why don't you come with me?" I asked.

"Fine," he said. "I could do combat art. I've always wanted to be a combat artist!" And that's how it all started.

With 1600 press people already in Saudi, and many of them kicking the sands of controversy into official Saudi faces, I knew it could be tough to get a visa. But I figured the Saudi government would respond if I had a little Pentagon backing. And how do you get the *Pentagon* to support you? By having key U. S. senators, the guys who appropriate the military dollars, in your corner. And how do you get the *Senate* on your side? By having their constituent newspapers, the folks who buy their ink by the barrel, suggest it to them.

So, before leaving Montana, I wrote a note to the 400 or so small town papers that subscribe to my weekly cartoon feature, *J.P. DOODLES*, asking them to write me "To Whom It May Concern" letters of support. By the time I'd arrived at Glenn's Ghost Fleet Gallery on the Outer Banks, nearly 50 letters were waiting. Most mentioned that a number of troops from their communities were serving in the Gulf, and many said they thought it would ease things considerably at home if their cartoonist were permitted to go over there and do his work.

"While war is not a laughing matter, Barry's insightful cartoons can make it more tolerable to the average small town American," wrote Michele Bartmess, editor of the paper in Murray, Utah. Murray had already lost one of its marines to friendly fire.

I sent copies of Michele's letter and a dozen others to the senators who represented the states where the papers were published. Four senators wrote letters back, voicing their encouragement and offering whatever help they could provide.

I carried these letters to Washington, D.C., and asked the Public Affairs Department at the Pentagon to respond with one of its own. Then, with all the above in hand, I visited the Saudi Consulate. In less than a week, I had my visa.

*Glenn called the Army offering to "re-up,"
but they turned him down.*

Funny, isn't it, how often you'll think you're going someplace for a particular reason, then end up going there for a different reason entirely. At the outset of this odyssey, my plan was to draw 100 cartoons about a projected 100-day war, something akin to Bill Mauldin's classics from WWII. I'd send these cartoons back to my papers to give my readers a small town slant on the war's progress.

But the Ground War lasted only 100 hours. It was over before I could even get there, so somewhere in the process another plan developed. The result was this book.

Sometimes I'd just hitch a ride with the first Arab
gentleman who offered me one.

During my five weeks in the war theater, I travelled throughout Saudi Arabia and Kuwait, and sailed the Persian Gulf, collecting as broad a cross-section of war-related cartoon ideas and anecdotes as possible. I arrived just after the fighting ended and found myself in what pilots would call "a target-rich environment," with the troops still deployed in place, tensions eased, and good humor in abundance everywhere.

Right off, I distanced myself from "the press," choosing casual small group discussions over formal briefings and interviews. The powers-that-be must have figured I was pretty harmless, being just a small town cartoonist, because they let me "hang out" with the troops when and where I pleased.

The ideal setting for me to gather my material was in a field tent or bunker, around a tank or aircraft, or in a mess hall or crew quarters—often in the middle of the night. I'd select some characters from the outfit at hand and encourage them to tell me about the

3

funny and unusual stuff that happened as they fought against the Iraqis and against their own battle stress.

Transportation was frequently provided by the military. I caught rides in helos, C-130s, humvees, suburbans, and 2 1/2–ton trucks. Sometimes I'd fly along for the ride with the *big* guys—you know, CNN, ABC, NBC, and CBS—but, where they'd only stick around for two or three hours, grab a few video "bites" for the day's news, then split, I'd stay for days, searching out the "real" stuff a book like this requires.

Sometimes, when military transport wasn't available, I'd just stand out on a Saudi freeway and thumb a ride with the first Arab gentleman who offered me one. As a result, I was able to do two or three lengthy interviews every 24 hours, covering a wide range of units from all branches of the U. S. services deployed there, as well as from folks in the Kuwaiti underground and the British Army.

So here you have it, my contribution to the war effort: *This Ain't Hell...But You Can See It From Here!* Hope you enjoy it.

On Military Humor

You run the gamut of emotions, up and down, during wartime. The pressures are unique to this pursuit. I mean, the board member that's got the million dollar deal? Sure he's got his pressures, but bring him out here! It's child's play next to a night carrier landing after you've just been out and had a dozen missiles fired at you, and know you're going again three hours after you land, even though you've had only two hours of sleep in the last thirty-six. I could walk you around the ship and introduce you to a hundred guys that have done that in the last month.

The pressure relief valve, if you perfectly define it, is *irreverent* humor. This encompasses all black humor and foul humor. *The dirtier, the fouler, the more irreverent, the better*. Nothing is sacred. We make the running gag:

"Geez, how's your wife doing?"

"Oh, she's okay."

"Is she having any problems getting the tank tracks out of the yard?"

That's the tank tracks from the marines who are in there while you're away on cruise. Then there's the old comeback, "No, it's okay, I left my boots out."—meaning they'd rather shine boots than screw, so that keeps your wife from getting laid by all the marines.

And, as aviators, our big gag is the Harrier marks— you know, the burn marks from the Harriers doing vertical take-offs in your backyard.

This is the black humor that, if you mentioned it to your neighbor, he'd probably deck you. But to us, it's a form of gallows humor which is unique to the military. The same guy who cusses at you one second is crying on your shoulder the next, and, three minutes later, both of you are in the wardroom having lunch and laughing your asses off.

Comdr. "Bug" Roach
Senior Air Wing Landing Signal Officer
USS *Ranger*

The Shield

Training was hell.
The war was nothing!

Lt. John Butler
595th Medical Company (Clearing)

Incoming

The first joke I picked up on my Gulf War Zone tour was told to me by a British airline captain aboard Saudia Flight 028 somewhere over the Mediterranean.

"You won't get it until you've been there a while," he said. "What are the only two things that *work* in Saudi Arabia?"

It was so good to hear a woman's voice again!

I shot him a blank look, so he answered. "Patriots and expatriates!"

He was right. I didn't get it. Not till I'd spent a few days "in country" and saw for myself what his joke implied, that Saudi citizens don't work—at least "work" as defined by American blue collar standards. While the Saudi people do own and manage businesses, and administrate government offices, it's the expatriates who labor in Saudi society. Sri Lankans and Bangladeshis drive the cabs. Indians and Filipinos wait the tables. Europeans and Americans handle the skilled and technical services. Et cetera.

As it happened, my first full-blown cartoon idea was inspired by one of these "expats," an American civilian contracted by Sikorsky Helicopter to teach the Saudi Army about helo maintenance.

He was waiting for a friend outside customs in the Riyadh Airport lobby. "What did you think of the war?" I asked.

"I was really glad when our troops came over," he said.

I figured this was because his base, King Khalid Military City, sat just below the Iraqi border in central Saudi, and he was afraid Saddam would attack.

But then he added, "It was *so* good to hear a woman's voice again!"

Once more I didn't get it. Of course, I hadn't learned yet about a Saudi custom relating to women—how the indigenous females there are forbidden to talk to men in public, particularly young, virile American men. Quite naturally then, after two years on the job, this helo guy was absolutely thrilled to see our forces arrive and to hear the chatter of our gals-in-arms.

Thanks to a series of revelations like those above, before long I had a pretty good feel for the culture shock our troops experienced as they deployed in Saudi to fight Saddam.

Just a Warning

The clash of Saudi and American cultures represented just one of the problems the war effort faced at the outset of Operation Desert Shield. The age-old rivalries between our military branches also added their share of confusion to the rapid Gulf deployment.

Since time immemorial, there's been a fiercely competitive spirit at play between the branches. And, though in recent years officialdom has demanded better inter-service coordination and the elimination of old feuds, the rivalries still raged in the Persian Gulf.

When the 19 Apache helicopters of the 101st Airborne (Air Assault) Division's 1st Battalion, 101st Aviation Regiment, arrived at King Fahd International on August 20, they were the only "tank killers" in the Gulf Theater, and therefore the only real deterrent to keep Saddam's vast armored legions from sweeping over the entire Arabian Peninsula.

Fully aware of this, Lt. Col. Dick Cody, the 1st Battalion's commanding officer, saw to it that his Apaches were off-loaded quickly from the C-5As and made fully operational within hours.

But, as high priority as their mission might be, the 1st Battalion didn't get the red carpet treatment at Fahd that other incoming units received. According to WO1 Jerry Orsbern:

> Some of the Aviation Brigade's headquarters people were on the same airplane that I was on. The first thing they did when we landed was jump off the airplane, get in an air-conditioned bus and ride away. I don't know where they went, but after that they always looked well-fed and showered.

According to Cody, the higher HQ people all had cars and nice living quarters. "All of *our* troops, including me as battalion commander, slept underneath our aircraft on the tarmac for three nights."

The U.S. Air Force had arrived first at Fahd and had taken charge of overall base operations. This set the stage for some classic inter-service dramatics when the Army Apaches flew in. Cody smiled as he recalled it:

> We thought we owned it. But when we got here, the Air Force owned it. They wanted us to park on one side, we wanted to park on the other. It was like an Oklahoma land grab. I can remember leading the flight in. They had some Air Force guy up in the tower tellin' me to land over there, on the other runway, but I'd already decided I was gonna park here. So that's what we did, and they got very irate about it. They moved aircraft in all around us—but once we got here, we never moved. Much to the chagrin of the Air Force. They *wanted* this prime ramp space.

Cody knew he had to secure some permanent quarters for his people, but it was slim pickings. King Fahd International was still five years from completion and, though the runways were finished, the terminal itself was just a shell of concrete slabs, plasterboard and steel. Cody found his solution in the airport parking garage.

"My pilots fly a fifteen-million-dollar Apache, the world's greatest attack aircraft, and the accommodations that we had was a four-story parking garage. Everybody had their own parking stall—compact or luxury—it didn't matter."

In spite of his unit's lack of perks, Cody didn't complain. It was partly out of a sense of duty. He knew right from the git-go that anytime something happened along the border, the chain of reaction would come down directly to them, and they would have to respond instantly. And it was partly a matter of pride. This was what was to be expected in war, and Cody wanted everyone to know his people were up to it.

"We lived in the parking garage the entire time. But you knew where the Air Force was. They had the air-conditioned billets. Didn't make any difference what rank they were, they all had billets."

Once Cody had gotten his people room, he set about getting them board.

"The Air Force, our brothers-in-arms and comrades-in-combat, had food catered in three mess halls," he said. "All we had were MREs (Meals Ready-to-Eat)."

"We had plenty of MREs," Orsbern noted. "It's just that the menu was limited and you kinda got tired of 'em after awhile—after seven or eight months!"

"So," said Cody, "we worked out a deal where we could eat with the Air Force. But, then, our numbers grew so quickly that they put signs up sayin', '101st NOT WELCOME HERE'. So we went back to eating MREs."

The unguided missile hit the Air Force, and seven
of their bird colonels were just livid. I told 'em,
"Don't give us any more grief about this ramp!"

"And care packages from home," Orsbern added. "The people back home really helped us survive by sending those packages."

The Air Force, still bristling over Cody's "squatter's rights" grab on the ramp, also took issue with his tactic of fully-armed Apaches so close to the terminal. But Cody explained:

> When we landed here, all our guys were so afraid that we'd be caught short before we went to war, that we loaded up all our Apaches.
> At the International Airport, from August 23rd on, my Apaches had two hundred Hellfire missiles loaded on them. Locked and loaded, ready to go north the first time Saddam stepped across the line.

Still, every day, one Air Force officer or another would come around to bitch at him about the danger posed by his Apaches. "What if those things went off?" they'd ask.

> I told 'em, "There's no way. I mean, you have seven buttons to push before you can even get that missile off there. Don't worry about it. Hell, we're all experts on this thing!"

But the Air Force continued to harass him, complaining about the ramp, the Hellfires, and even the blowing dust from the helo blades.

And then it happened—what Cody later described as a "functional check of weapon systems."

> In October, one of my kids was runnin' up the aircraft. We'd been flying those things every day, powering them up. He went out there, ran it up, and was just checking something, when suddenly the missile came off the rail. It flew between our Army helicopters and landed in an ammo supply point that belonged to the Air Force. And blew it up.
> I mean, it was an unguided missile, it could have gone off into the desert. It could have gone anywhere. But what's it do? It hits the Air Force.
> Seven 06's, full bird Air Force colonels, came by and they were just *livid*, yelling at me like I did it on purpose! And I told 'em, "Hey, guys, that's just the first warning shot. Don't give us any more grief about being on this ramp!"

Brothers-in-Arms

The parries and thrusts of the Army aviators versus the Air Force pretty well typified the rivalry I found everywhere. About the only consensus reached in the Persian Gulf among the American military branches was the general agreement that air power "won" the war. This conclusion was rarely challenged, especially by the infantry, tankers and other ground forces who were eternally grateful for the "softening up" that the air forces provided.

"I hope the airboys are getting enough congrats," said Gunny John D. Cornwell of the 8th Tank Battalion, 2nd Marine Division (8th Tanks, 2 MARDIV). "We woulda kicked ass *without* 'em but, because of what they did, we didn't take any casualties."

Beyond that, however, it was open season on the "brothers-in-arms." No matter who I visited, the conversation inevitably worked its way around to "they"—meaning "that other branch." So it was when I sailed the Gulf aboard the USS *Ranger*, and Comdr. "Bug" Roach, the carrier's senior air wing landing signal officer, enlightened me on the differences between the way the Navy built air bases and the way "they"—meaning the Air Force—did it:

> When *they* go about building an air station, the first thing they build is the officers' club, the exchange, and the barracks. They build all of the infrastructure, then start on good hangars with lots of ramp area. *Then* they start to build the runways.
>
> And because everything is underbid, by the time they're done with the first 2000 ft. of runway, they're out of money. So they go to Congress and say, "We need more money to finish up."
>
> And the Congress says, "We can't *give* you any more money."
>
> Then the Air Force says, "Oh, okay. Well, let us know when you can, and we"ll move into our new air base."
>
> Congress says, "Wait a minute! You can't move in?"
>
> "Hell no!" replies the Air Force. "We haven't got a runway!"
>
> "Oh, jeezus! Okay!" cries Congress, and they have a big emergency session to give the Air Force the money. This is not a joke, but it's not oversimplifying it. This is the way it happens. They get more money than the Navy does

*A marine corporal reported to his CO
with good news and bad news.*

every damn year, because they've got a better lobby. They know how to play the system.

The first thing the *Navy* builds are brand new, beautiful, double runways. And gorgeous ramp areas. By the time they get around to things like barracks, base officers' quarters, and the officers' club, they run out of money. Congress says, "Well, hey, why don't you operate awhile? And we'll try to get you something *next* fiscal year, or the year after!"

I hope you don't think I'm picking on the Air Force. That's sure not my intent. Besides, nobody could possibly pick on the Air Force as well as it picks on itself.

Take the way the Fightin' 69th at Al Kharj spoke of its comrades in the 511th at King Fahd. The 69th flew swift F-16s, which often were assigned the same sort of missions as the 511th's slower A-10s, prompting Kharj's Falcons to tease Fahd's Warthogs mercilessly.

When asked about the A-10's ability to "take a hit," Falcon commanding officer Lt. Col. Bob "Boomer" Hill said, "It's because they're so well trained. Instead of a simulator, they just stick 'em in a trash can and bang on the outside of it!"—a reference to the Warthog's round titanium cockpit tub.

A bunch of Air Force guys were making snide comments about Marines, and the fight was on!

Describing the difference in top-end air speeds between Falcons and Warthogs, Boomer said, "The F-16s carry a map for a single mission. The A-10s carry calendars."

"Tankers slow down for A-10s during mid-air refueling," joined in Falcon driver Mike "Buckeye" Sweeney.

"Birds fly into them from behind," added Boomer.

The Warthogs returned the fire. According to them, "The F-16's motto is, *One pass, haul ass!*"—alluding to the Falcon's reputed fragility.

But, all in all, nobody got picked on as much as the Navy. Even

Even **Doonesbury** *poked fun at their access
to daily showers and air-conditioning.*

Garry Trudeau took a shot at the Navy in his comic strip, *Doonesbury*, poking fun at their access to daily showers and air-conditioning.

This irritated a lot of sailors, who felt that Trudeau, who draws from the lap of penthouse luxury in New York and has never served aboard ship—or served *anywhere else* for that matter—was giving them a bum rap.

Comdr. Bug Roach agreed. "Screw Garry Trudeau. You *cannot* be too good to yourself on cruise."

The Navy also usually got the brunt of it when inter-service rivalry spawned inter-service *thievery*. As the old service adage goes, "The Marines steal from the Army, the Army steals from the Air Force, and *everybody* steals from the Navy."

But, in the Gulf, the most highly touted inter-service theft was a Marines-from-Army heist. According to Samuel Watts of the HQ Battalion, 2nd Marine Division (HQ Bn., 2 MARDIV), "The Marine Corps did a pretty good job. We didn't have enough vehicles, so the

Army came up missing about twenty." Some say it was more like fifty.

Another marine added that he'd heard the guy responsible for this beyond-the-call-of-duty manuever was up for an under-the-table Marine commendation.

As Glenn Eure, my traveling buddy in Saudi, would say, "Marines will never run out of trucks, as long as the Army keeps parking them!"

Of all the branches, the Marines probably picked on their comrades-in-combat better than all the rest—at least, more uniformly than the others. About the Army, Capt. John "The Vein" Kostecki of the 8th Tanks said, "The best thing a marine can say about an Army guy is nothin'."

Another marine added, "The Iraqis heard the Army was coming, and they were ready to fight. Then they heard the Marines were coming instead, and they said, 'Okay, let's get those white towels out.'"

Naturally, the Army would counterattack. Lt. Col. Michael T. Johnson, of the 2nd Armored Division's infamous "Tiger Brigade," told me: "We're proud of the Marines. As a matter of fact, back in November, we were concerned that they weren't getting the proper supplies or being treated properly, so we were fixing to have a Christmas clothing drive for them. We figured they weren't getting uniforms because they weren't wearing any! They were all wearing rags on their heads and T-shirts."

Army guys would also refer to marines as "self-propelled sand-bags."

As disparaging as this may seem, it was a long way from what Saddam was telling Iraqis about the Marines. "To be a Marine," he told his forces, "you have to kill one of your own family. And eat them!"

Later, when I talked with an 8th Tanker who'd heard of Saddam's accusations, he responded with, "Yeah, they're good! Yum-yum!"

The Marines also chewed on the Air Force. Sgt. Ernie Grafton, with HQ Bn., 2 MARDIV, said he hated to go onto Air Force bases. "The Air Force has so many generals, I'm always saluting. My arm gets tired!"

And later I was told the story in which a Marine corporal reported to his CO during the war with good news and bad news.

"Sir," he said, "the good news is, the Air Force has a big tank column pinned down just north of here. The bad news is, the tanks are *ours*."

The Navy and the Marine Corps share a historical kinship, but the Marines held nothing back on them either. Out in the field, when a marine had his first MRE bowel movement, he often referred to it as "giving birth to a nine-pound sailor."

And, like Trudeau, the Marines made considerable fun of Navy air-conditioning. "Must be like Monte Carlo," one scruffy marine told me inside his raggedy-ass bunker in Kuwait.

In reprisal, the Navy always delighted in showing up the Marines

***The air-conditioned canvas billets were
a total mystery to the Marines.***

where they were most vulnerable. When the Seabees were building Fleet Hospital 15, outside Al Jubail, members of the Marine detachment assigned to defend the facility were ordered to help put up the Navy tents. While the USMC could teach the USN a great deal about living in the desert, the Navy had to instruct the grunts on "temper tents." These double-walled, air-conditioned canvas billets were a total mystery to the marines, who'd never had to mess with anything more complex than field tents or sandbagged holes in the ground.

Still, there were times when the blood flowing through sailors and marines was thicker than the Gulf water. Bug Roach remembered once when a bunch of Air Force pilots were knocking the Marines while in the company of some naval aviators:

> A bunch of Air Force guys came down from Clark Air Base and were making snide comments about Marines. A bunch of sailors took exception and jumped 'em. The fight was on!
> It's okay for *us* to call 'em bastards, but it's *not* okay for some Air Force weenie to call 'em bastards!

However, in spite of this kind of close-air support, the Marines kept picking away at the Navy. They just weren't happy unless they were waging relentless attacks on somebody's reputation, even that of their own comrades.

The Civil War erupted anew within the 8th Tank marines, as the Johnny Reb companies rallied against the Yankee units in their battalion.

Captain Kostecki explained. "You had Alpha Co. from Kentucky. You had a unit out of South Carolina, and part of it from Tallahassee. But the headquarters was out of New York State. So you had the Yankees trying to lead the southern boys. And we were always bumping heads."

Gunny Cornwell grinned in agreement. "There were two tank companies forward and one tank company back. The company that stayed back was the Yankees, and all the southern boys were forward. We won the fuckin' war for 'em, and we ain't letting 'em forget it!"

Before long, the Gulf War brass could've easily identified with General Eisenhower's comment in WWII—"Isn't it enough that we have the enemy to fight?"—but the average Joe took it in stride.

As one Seabee said, "It comes with the job."

In Country

"Why is the Saudi Arabian flag green, when there's not one green thing on this whole fucking peninsula?" wrote an Air Force loadmaster in his squadron's "Dufer Book" (journal). This airman was just venting a little of the frustration many troops shared over being deployed to the climatically hostile, culturally bewildering Gulf War Zone.

While some troops would carry this frustration with them throughout their Gulf tours, most gradually began to re-orient themselves to their new environs, often with *imaginative* perspectives.

Lt. John Butler, of the Army's 595th Medical Company (Clearing), remembered the process of adjustment for his outfit:

> We'd only been here a month or two when we started to learn the rules of the country. If you drove around enough and you saw the little towns along the roads, it might have reminded you of someplace down in the middle of Mexico, or out in parts of the midwest. Little places that were just shacks and really run-down shanty towns.
>
> There would be a few shops in what I guess they saw as a plaza, with a few camels parked out in front and, maybe, a Mercedes-Benz. Once I was driving out there and I saw these two guys talking between a camel and Mercedes, and I thought, I wonder if they're talking about trading. Or if the guy with the car is asking the other guy if he's seen his keys.

It took some troops awhile to get their balance under these startlingly new conditions, literally so for SSgt. Raymond Howard of the 4th Marines, 2 MARDIV:

> I woke up the morning after the night we'd arrived in Saudi. I reached down to pick my glasses up, but I broke 'em.
>
> Then I tried to adjust my shoulder holster, but wound up cuttin' it in two, with buckles flying everywhere.
>
> Next I went outside to the head, came back inside, tripped and did a triple somersault.

Master Gunnery Sgt. Larry Kennedy, Howard's superior, who'd

*It was more important to have polished boots
than to concentrate on training.*

watched the staff sergeant struggle for his bearings, joked, "Since he was gonna be my assistant maintenance chief, I hated to think how he was with machinery!"

The military has always been big on training. But for some troops, who were dealing with the reality of war for the first time and, therefore, genuinely concerned about their preparedness, Gulf training often seemed to lag. Sgt. Michael Baldasarre of the 6th Marines, 2 MARDIV, wished at times that the spit and polish would have given way to more critical areas of training, like showing him how to stay *alive*:

> There were administrative problems. We weren't concentrating on the war. It was more important to have polished boots and a good haircut than it was to concentrate on training for what was about to happen.
> Not to say I'm a brilliant person or that I've had a lot

of experience, but I think it was because a lot of the leaders had never been in a war-type situation and, when we arrived, they still ran things like we did on our training missions back in the states at peacetime.

If other aspects of training seemed to lag, it was not so with Nuclear-Biological-Chemical (NBC) warfare training, where the troops and their equipment were constantly being checked out in drills.

It was during one such drill that a female Army officer sounded the clarion call of the woman-at-arms, and made clear to military males exactly what they could expect from the "gentler sex" in this war.

One cold desert morning, the lady captain led her people in for a test of their NBC equipment, to see whether or not it would leak when the troops went to "MOPP-4" (fully geared up for a gas attack).

A male NBC specialist broke out a water hose and wet down the MOPP-4ed troops, using the water to test for leaks. But he didn't just spray them all thoroughly. He *doused* them in a blinding, freezing, soaking torrent—till the soldiers were visibly shaking from the cold.

Their captain was irate. The test wasn't supposed to be comfortable, but the NBC guy was overdoing it, and obviously enjoying himself in the process. She charged over to him, put her face right in his, and hollered, *"Fuck with my troops again, and I'll show you the true meaning of the word 'BITCH'!"*

Without Wheels

American teenagers have always been well-versed in the lines that work to pry the car keys loose from the folks. But no teen ever had a better line than the one Will Bain used.

When Saddam invaded Kuwait and threatened to roll across the

"Sure, you can borrow the car," Mrs. Bain said. "But you'll have to come to Dharan and get it!"

entire Arabian Peninsula, it meant something special to LCpl. Will Bain, stationed then with the Marines at Camp LeJeune, North Carolina. Will's parents, Gene and Katie Bain, were currently living and working in Saudi Arabia, as they had been for years. In fact, Will had grown up there.

So, naturally, when Saddam made his move, this young man

received a whole lot more attention than usually was accorded a lowly lance corporal. Suddenly he was cast into the limelight as Lejeune's resident expert on all things Gulf-related, regularly briefing groups of officers, including division intelligence, and fellow grunts on the lay of the land, the climate, the people and their customs.

At this time there was a mad scramble on to get troops and equipment in place, to deter further Iraqi aggression. But often the soldiers arrived in Saudi well ahead of their materiel, or vice versa. Sometimes the two would arrive in country simultaneously, only at different locations. Confusion was frequently the order of the day.

When Will and his Marine advance party showed up at Al Jubail, they were loaded onto a Saudi school bus and driven out to their desert campsite, only to find it consisted of one shelter-half and an empty five-gallon water jug. "Hell no!" said Will's commanding officer, and he ordered his people back on the bus and returned to Jubail.

It was then that the CO learned it wasn't just tents that were in short supply in Saudi, but tactical vehicles, too. When he asked for his "Hummer"—the Marine nickname for the Humvee—he was told it hadn't arrived yet. Since today's rapid deployment marine is about as useless without wheels as an old horse cavalryman was without his mount, the CO turned to Lance Corporal Bain for help.

"You're the Saudi expert," he said. "So what do I do now?"

"No problem, sir," the young man answered. "Let me call my mom." And that's exactly what he did.

"Sure, you can borrow the car," Mrs. Bain said. "But you'll have to come to Dharan and get it yourself—I want to see you!"

So Will and his CO hitched a ride south to the Bain's place in Dharan. And for the first two weeks of their deployment, this particular detachment of marines was commanded from the front seat of a family station wagon.

The Weather Girl

The CO of the USS *Ranger*, Capt. Ernest Christensen, Jr., had been farsighted enough back in San Diego to install the right equipment on his aircraft carrier to pick up CNN. So, as he and his men sailed toward the Gulf, they kept up to the minute on all the latest news.

The weather girl closed by saying she wished all the boys could see how well the panties fit.

And what was the crew's favorite CNN attraction?

It wasn't Peter Arnett, though Peter did get high ratings later on for his great play-by-play as the *Ranger* aviators pummeled Bagdad.

Nor was it any of the military analysts who offered the flyers advice on the right way to win the war.

No, the big hit was the weather girl. Everything stopped aboard the *Ranger* when Valerie Voss did weather. Throughout the ship, in ready rooms and work lockers, in wardrooms and command control centers, every time CNN broke to a commercial, expectations soared— Valerie might be next!

And, when Ms. Voss did appear, she held the sailors in the palms of her hands. Her long, warm, supple hands.

Though other CNN females had their followings, too, Valerie was undeniably the "Ranger Girl"—to the point that one A-6 Intruder squadron, VA-155, sent her a special invitation, proposing that she be at their Whidbey Island, Washington, airstrip to meet them as they flew in from the Gulf.

To sweeten the deal, the flyers stuck a pair of black lace panties, adorned with their "Silver Foxes" emblem, into the envelope with the invite.

Imagine their ecstasy when Valerie actually wrote back. While her letter said she probably couldn't make the date, she promised to try. Then she closed by saying how much she appreciated the panties and wished all the boys could see how well they fit.

I understand the captain ordered the hot water shut off aboard ship till the squadron had finished its evening showers.

Bird's-Eye at War

Abrams tanks, Bradley fighting vehicles, Apache helicopters, and Patriot and Tomahawk missiles. What did all these things have in common? They were all battlefield-tested in the Gulf War. And so were the MREs, which *officially* stood for "Meals-Ready-to-Eat"— though many troops preferred other interpretations of the acronym, such as "Meals Rejected by Ethiopians" and "Meals Refusing to Exit," just to name a couple.

"I bet they're pretty good," I suggested to one soldier, "if you eat them when you're really hungry."

"That's exactly the *wrong* time to eat them!" he replied.

They can't be *that* bad, I thought, reflecting back to my army days in the mid-'60s, when all you had for groceries in the field were C-rations—those little olive drab tins that required some real handy work with a P-38 GI can opener or a fixed bayonet just to get at the food. Then, it was this jellied, greasy, lumpy concoction of mystery meat and cold gravy.

So, naturally, when I first heard the Gulf War troops gripe about the MREs, it seemed to me they were being pretty picky. After all, the MREs offered a great-sounding menu of 10 tantalizing entrees, such as "Ham Slices in Natural Juices," "Meatballs in Spicy Tomato Sauce," "Chicken A La King," and "Ham Omelet." And with each entree the troops got a yummy side order of something like "Potatoes Au Gratin."

All of this came vacuum-packed in heavy, brown plastic pouches, like "Bird's-Eye at War," which made them a whole lot easier to open and to pack around than the C-ration cans. Moreover, the MREs were accompanied by little, high-tech sleeve heaters—or, they were *supposed* to have these heaters—which slipped over the main courses and, with the addition of a little water, provided *hot* chow in a matter of minutes.

But, maybe the troops were right, and maybe I was just suckered in by the novelty of the new MREs. It sure did appear that the military itself had its doubts about the appeal of these meals, judging from the ever present bottles of "Texas Pete" or Tabasco sauce, miniature versions of which were packed with every MRE entrée.

The military's regard for the MREs seemed suspect again when I learned about the truck loaded with them that crashed in Iraq.

"I bet MREs are pretty good," I suggested, "if you eat them when you're really hungry."

Sgt. Michael "Mickey" Malloy, of the 595th Medical Company (Clearing), described the scene:

> On the way up to our site, we noticed an overturned eighteen-wheeler with MREs spilled everywhere. I don't think the Army cared about them at all. There were weeks' worth of meals, a rack total of thousands of dollars. I guess the Army must have felt bad for the Iraqi people who weren't eating, and left them the food.

While some soldiers may have interpreted this as a humanitarian gesture to hungry people, others simply saw it as "good riddance."

Also included with the MRE main courses were a variety of snack items, such as cocoa, Kool-aid, fruit cake and pound cake, coffee, chewing gum, M&Ms, a few pretty tough saltine crackers, and some *very* tough oatmeal cookies.

The troops really prized the cocoa and Kool-aid. They added the cocoa to their coffee, creating "Coco-Joe" or "Moco," the hot drink of preference throughout the war zone. But cocoa hadn't always been a standard MRE item, and only after considerable "suggesting" by the troops was it inserted into the meal packets.

The Kool-aid was added to the abundant bottled water, killing its chlorinated taste and odor, and soothing the yearnings for soda pop when soda was in short supply.

The M&Ms were only found in some of the meal packets such as "Chicken A La King," which popularized them as menu selections. So, even though an entrée like "Chicken A La King" might rate near rockbottom on the one-to-ten "what's appetizing" scale, it was feverishly sought after—if only for its M&Ms. You'll appreciate this sacrifice better once you hear Sgt. Hamilton "Oakie" Rigney's view on "Corned Beef Hash," another of those entrées chosen to accompany the candy:

> The MREs that we had were the newer ones. When I first ate them, I took a particular liking to "Corned Beef Hash." I thought it tasted pretty good. But I was eating it in the dark.
>
> In the morning, I was scrounging through the MREs for some breakfast, and particularly looking for "Corned Beef Hash." I found it, and I opened it up. Another person was telling me, "Ew! Yuk! You like 'Corned Beef Hash'?"
>
> "Yeah," I said. "This stuff tastes pretty good!"
>
> So I opened up and I started eating it. Now, this was in the light, so I finally looked at it, and started noticing pieces of heart and veins. This particular "Corned Beef Hash" had mostly just veins in it, and portions of cow hearts. It grossed me out and, ever since then, I've never eaten another "Corned Beef Hash."

As for the infamous oatmeal cookies, they were so hard the troops found them useless, except for hammering nails or as something deadly to toss at the Iraqis when they ran out of standard-issue ordnance.

Last but not least, also included with the MREs, in "Accessory Packet A," was the all important toilet paper—but it was the John Wayne variety. "Rough, tough and it don't take shit off nobody!" was how one marine described it.

In an effort to enlighten his family on the joys of MRE cuisine, a sergeant in the 1st Marine Division (1 MARDIV) mailed an "Omelet and Ham" home, scribbling the following note on the package:

> For best results, eat cold. Tastes much better when served with a chilled white wine.

Still, tasty or not, the MREs were hoarded away, if for no other reason than in the hope that someday they could be *swapped* for something more appealing—say, perhaps, for *French* rations. It was rumored the French meals were Continental classics from France's premier chefs, often seasoned in wine sauce and served with Perrier water. But, ooo la la, they were neither cheap nor easy to find.

Supposedly, the going exchange rate in the Gulf was *five* MREs for *one* French ration—though, it's really difficult to imagine that the sophisticated French palate would desire five of *anything* that the provincial American taste buds had flatout rejected. Besides, some Frenchmen had already had an experience with American food under their belts—one too many, as Maj. William Alden Smith, flight surgeon with the 511th Tactical Fighter Squadron, discovered:

> They were eating at the American chow hall. I could tell they were in a morbid state of depression, because they were eating American food. I wondered if they'd need electric convulsive psychotherapy!

Regardless, the Americans made frequent attempts to get their hands on the French meals. Army Specialist Victor Stark, of the 82nd Airborne, approached a guy in a French uniform one day and asked, "You-o want-o to trade-o for MRE-o's?"

Turns out the guy was a French Legionnaire from Atlanta, Georgia. "What th' hell ya'll tryin' t' say?" he asked.

The Shitters

During the Saudi deployment, some troops were called upon to perform a number of basic tasks absolutely crucial to camp operations. One of the most basic of these was servicing the field toilets.

Field toilets, known affectionately by the Marines as "shitters," were usually found in first echelon camps just behind the tactical frontlines. In the absence of plumbing, even the porta-potty variety, 55 gallon drums were cut in half and slid from the rear under the toiletseat benches of the wooden and screen structures. Most of these shitters were four-holers, requiring four of the half-drums.

Once a shitter was used to capacity, the drums were pulled out and dragged a safe distance away from the structure. Then they were doused with JP-5 jet fuel and burned. At least that's how it was *supposed* to be done.

One fine Saudi day, a gunnery sergeant ordered a lance corporal to "go burn the shitter." Lance corporals have always been scared to death of the gunnies. So when a gunny would say, "Jump!" a lance corporal wouldn't even ask "How high?"—he'd just start jumping.

And that's just how it was with the lance corporal in question. Reacting out of pure fear and responding with absolute thoughtlessness, he leaped over to the fuel dump, grabbed some JP-5 and poured it directly into the four shitter holes. Then he threw in a match and jumped clear.

WHOOOSH! went the shitter.

In an instant the gunny was hauling ass in his direction, primed and ready to blow. *"Lance corporal,"* he hollered, *"what in the hell have you done?"*

"Just what you said, Gunny. I burned the shitter."

"Lance corporal," roared the gunny, *"don't do what I SAY—do what I MEAN!"*

Obviously, burning the shitters was never an enviable job. Yet as Cpl. R.N. "Frenchy" Gravel of the Helicopter Marine Medium (HMM) Squadron 261 pointed out, somebody had to do it:

> In Jubail, it wasn't so bad. You got little fiberglass boxes. When they overflowed, a pump truck came in and they sucked out the "ha-ha."

He essentially had a day off, a good deal.
Until Top Walker found out about it.

In Lonesome Dove it was different, because we didn't have the trucks. We had what we called a "working party." Usually the senior guy picked the lowest troops for the "shit detail." Or he picked guys who messed up the day before. But when he arrived in the morning, everybody squatted down, thinking, *Oh, I hope he doesn't see me!*

He walked up and said, "I need a volunteer!" You know that nobody raised their arm. So he picked you.

So you'd go up to the shitter. You tried to be careful not to smell it, putting your finger up your nose. And then you pulled the barrels out, added jet fuel, and burned it away. Usually takes a couple hours. It's about like they said in the movie, *Platoon*—"the literal meaning of shit detail."

Though not an enviable job, some of the chosen tried to turn it into one, as Lt. Victor "Schtick" Duniec, a pilot for HMM-261 explained:

I remember one morning when Top Walker picked Corporal McCarthy to burn shit. McCarthy had been late for formation, so he'd volunteered unwittingly. But being the marine full of ingenuity that he is, McCarthy decided that he'd make a day of it.

He pulled out the "honey buckets," put the JP-5 in them, and lit 'em. Then, he took out his lounge chair and his Sony Walkman, stripped down to his shorts, and started sunbathing. He essentially had a day off, a good deal.

Until Top Walker found out about it, and said, "No, you're gonna *stand* all day and *stir* it until it's all done burning!" So the next day he was out there again, stirring it with a stick.

Mail Call

There were no phone centers on the fleet, so mail was the only connection with home for sailors in the Gulf. Aware of this, the powers-that-be made certain that the Navy received its share of "To Any Serviceman" letters and packages. Maybe *more* than its share.

When the USS *Ranger* put in at Subic Bay in the Philippines enroute to the Gulf, 10,000 lbs. of "To Any Serviceman" mail was waiting dockside. It warmed the hearts of the sailors to see this outpouring of support from back home. But it also threw one helluva big monkey wrench into the regular mail delivery system. Due to this tidal wave of "To Any Serviceman" mail, much of the mail the sailors wanted most—that from their families and friends—was buried in some warehouse ashore and delayed for weeks.

The soldiers, marines and airmen ashore in Saudi had their own problems with mail. When stories were published back home about shortages of certain necessities, the troops were inundated with these products—though usually these "shortages" really didn't exist.

At one point the word went out that lip balm and toilet tissue were in short supply. For weeks after, our troops were clawing through the bundles of Chapstick and cases of Charmin they didn't need, looking for the cookies and candy they *always* wanted.

Another interesting, though misguided, product to arrive was condoms. One mom explained, in the note she attached to a box of the things, that she'd heard the marines needed them to put over their gun barrels in order to keep the sand out. Since she didn't know how big his gun was, she sent along the magnum size, lubricated variety—just to be *safe*.

Most of the "To Any Serviceman" mail was full of heartfelt encouragement for the troops. People of all ages and from all walks of life wrote to convey their best wishes and their prayers. Often, these writers seemed motivated by a personal need to connect with someone "over there." Like the older lady who wrote one soldier that she'd lost her husband only a few months earlier. Her husband had served in "that same desert" during WWII, she said, and now she wanted to do something for this nice young troop like what someone had done for her man decades before. The soldier told me he wrote back to this lady and the two have since become real pen pals.

If a troop was lucky enough to be mentioned in the press back home, he or she would often be flooded by mail from local readers, many with amorous designs. If single and farsighted enough, soldiers could fill up their post-war dating calendars in a hurry.

Sometimes whole units would be adopted by service organizations, businesses, or schools. One squadron of Air Force F-15 pilots began hearing from a covey of exotic dancers at a Myrtle Beach nightclub. While most of the girls' letters reflected sincere and thoughtful expressions of concern, some also included outrageous pictures which could only have gotten past a Saudi censor who was asleep on the job.

Another airman at Al Kharj received pictures from his brother, some featuring local girls on the beach. Only, the brother, apparently respecting Saudi sensibilities, had taken a black felt marker and inked out all the exposed skin, except on the girls' faces. The airman said he appreciated his brother's good intentions, but still had to wonder, "Why bother, Bro?"

American schools were heavily involved in "To Any Serviceman" mail. Many troops took the kids' letters to heart, writing them back at length and often promising to visit this or that school when they returned.

A lot of the school letters were simply messages copied from classroom chalkboards. But others showed creative twists of mind. Like the one in which a young boy outlined in detail precisely how the marine aviators from HML-767 should sneak into Saddam's bunker and kill him. He even included a map.

Another flyer opened a letter from a school girl in New Orleans, where his unit is based, and found in it a humorous, though dubious, confidence builder. This aviator was then a part of the "PsyOps package," a highly hazardous operation. Day after day he'd fly at 150 feet above the Iraqi lines, while an interpreter on board would try to talk the enemy soldiers into surrendering from loudspeakers attached to the helicopter's skids. For a flyer, this was the supreme test of faith in your aircraft. But in her letter, the girl wrote of how proud she was that this marine was flying a Huey, "just like the one my grandpa used to fly."

A female Seabee at Fleet Hospital 15 near Al Jubail picked up a "To Any Sailor" letter one day. It was from a 12-year-old girl who began by introducing herself and her dog, Fifi, in the sweetest of all manners. But, in the second paragraph, her tone and her language changed radically: "When you catch Saddam, I want you to grab him by his ——— and cut the ——— off and shove it up his ———!" Although, she wrote it with all the blanks filled in.

Then, she shifted back to all sweetness and light in paragraph three, saying how she needed to get Fifi some milk now, but would remember our troops in her prayers.

You have to know something about the very real *fear* our troops experienced in the Gulf War to fully appreciate the dark humor in some of the kids' letters. Nearly everyone there, at one point or another, sincerely believed he or she was marked for death—that a

When stories were published about shortages, troops were inundated with products they really didn't need.

bullet or a SCUD or a land mine had his number on it, and was just lying in wait to target him personally.

That's why some of the letters from kids at home hit the troops—and their funnybones—so hard:

Dear Soldiers
I hope you don't get hurt or shot or blown up. God will help you untill you come back. That's if you do come back, whitch you will. Have a happy Hollaween dudes. Blow them out of the sky. Go for it.
Your friend, Frank

dear Soldiers
I hope you get home before christmas. before you die.
I hope you win but there is a chance you will die. have a
merry little christmas.
your friend, Tom
grade 3

Other "reassuring" messages from the kids to the troops included
such lines as:

If you guys lose the war, we're all doomed!

How does it feel knowing you might get shot down and
tortured?

You're so brave cuz you might get strung up and eaten.

We'll take you however you come back—if your arms
or legs are blown off or whatever. We'll still love you!

Then there was a delightful Valentine card, designed like a small
book, with page after page of little hearts—till, smack in the middle,
you hit a double-page spread crammed with explosions and the
inscription: "I hope Saddam blows up!"
Finally, there was a letter from a USS *Ranger* fan who knew *he*
was cool, and figured our Navy flyers must be, too:

To All of you crazy A-6 pilots,
My name is Jeff, and I live here on Coronado and I think
about you dudes alot. I live with a retired Marine so we
bullshit about the war quite a bit. Im not much of a
wrighter, but I can wish you the best and come home safe.
One last thing, be sure and fix youre Crosshairs on one of
those raghead motherfuckers for me. Fly safe.

Youre friend
Jeff
Party on!

P. S. Ill smoke a joint in youre name daily until its over.

War Dog Haircuts

Of all the threats that faced our troops prior to the outbreak of Desert Storm, the most *sinister* by far was "The In-Country Haircut"—sinister, because the individuals behind this fearful menace, the barbers, were *supposed* to be on our side.

You may already have read of the in-country haircut given to Tech Sgt. Tom Rominger, also known as "Zorro." He was the Air Force cartoonist whose work appeared in Gary Trudeau's *Doonesbury* comic strip. Tom's brutal brush with a barber received all kinds of notice throughout the theater. It even earned him a mention in *People* magazine's "The 15 Most Intriguing People (of the War)" issue.

According to *People*, one of Rominger's in-house cartoons, "depicting a less-than-macho military barber," caught the eye of the marine who regularly cut his hair.

The result was devastating, both to Tom's appearance and his pride.

I visited with Tom in Riyadh, just prior to the publication of the *People* report, and listened as he described, in excruciating detail, the strip the barber had shaved down the middle of his head—as barren as if it had been napalmed.

There were many other equally tragic, though less prominent, assaults by Gulf barbers—for instance, the one made on Lt. Jay "Flat Top" Todd, of the 69th Tactical Fighter Squadron (TFS) Werewolves. Everyone who knew Jay Todd also knew that he couldn't live without his flat top. It was his claim to fame. But, though Jay knew there weren't a lot of trained barbers in country, and though he usually subscribed to the squadron's maxim—*Never get your hair cut by someone who can't speak English*— he still chose to take his chances at one of the local shops.

Before long the scissors were flying, and so were the regrets. It wasn't pretty. But to fully appreciate the incident, you'd have to hear it from the squadron's Dufer Book, as I did. Jay read his own words:

> Go offensive early, just to clarify or give a reason for looking like I belong, not in the air with the flying Vipers, but on the ground with the jughead Marines.
>
> I'll tell you the complete story. *Before:* the perfect flat top, envied by all. *During:* my not-so-uneventful haircut appointment.

As he read, I glanced over his shoulder at some Dufer drawings, Jay Todd's self-portrait renditions of how his hair looked in the various stages of being cut to pieces. Jay looked up and, with a sad grin, he explained:

> Probably one of the worst feelings was to be sitting there in the barber shop and have him work on you for a few minutes, then step out in front, and go, "Oh, fuck!"
>
> It's kinda like a horse. When it breaks a leg, you gotta shoot it. Well, when he totally devastated my flat top, I had to *shear* it.
>
> Yeah, I wanted just a regular flat top, like I'd got for the last seven years. I actually grabbed the shears to show him how to do it, but he acted like he wasn't listening and went ahead and took it off. Then I found out he couldn't speak English and he didn't have a clue when cuttin' hair, but then it was too late!

One of the Werewolves who witnessed the horror described how the barber clicked the scissors awhile over Jay's flat top before he actually touched the hair. Obviously, this barber understood well the unnerving power of a threat *posed*, before a threat unleashed.

"The guy shoulda had a video camera on those shears," said another pilot. "It coulda won at the Gulf War Academy Awards!"

But, like in Zorro's case, most often it *was* an English-speaking barber and a fellow American troop who wreaked the havoc. Lt. Col. Rick Husty, of the Helicopter Marine Attack (HMA) Squadron 775 Coyotes, recalled his in-country haircut at the hands of another squadron flyer, Capt. Marc Richardson—AKA "The Mad Barber Mengele":

> I was here two days and wanted to get a haircut. "You ever cut hair before?" I asked him.
>
> "Oh yeah, I cut hair! No problem!"
>
> I sat down. So, he says he's cut hair—what, do I check for references? I didn't know!
>
> But the haircut was distinctive. It was like looking at a goat knot on your head. The fellas asked if you'd gone out in the field and a goat had got to ya!
>
> There's not a lot of mirrors here, so I couldn't confirm it for a day or so. But, it don't look bad in the mirror, from the front. It's the bowl cut in the back. Four or five officers had the same cut, and you knew *exactly* where it came from.
>
> I knew as soon as I walked in the terminal, people would start staring, like, "Oh my god!" *Die lauschenshowers* were next!

That was the first "accident" he'd ever had! Right now he's giving phenomenal haircuts. But the first month or so, it was really nip and tuck—it was the brave man who'd go first.

Word of the "Mad Barber Mengele" spread quickly among the Coyote personnel. And, for a while, when you walked over to the maintenance shop, you'd see the following sign:

WAR DOG HAIRCUTS

High and Mighty. . . . . 50¢
Ricki Recon . . . . 75¢
All others . . . . . buck and a half

"If you can't stop the bleeding, the haircut's free."

But the most sinister of *all* sinister haircuts was given before its victim even left the states—meaning, I suppose, that the culprit could've been shot as a saboteur, had he not been the HML-767's new flight surgeon. Capt. Bruce "Goose" Heim, of the 767 Nomads, gave me his account:

It was the night we were leaving Cherry Point, the place where we got on the big C-5s. The four-hour wait turned into a ten-hour wait, and we were just sittin' in the terminal. Then I saw that Doc Van Mask had a pair of hair clippers.

He was the replacement flight surgeon and had only been with us for a week or so before we deployed. Now, one would assume that, being a military flight surgeon, as well as a ER room surgeon in San Antonio, he'd have good hands and a lot of skills. And then you see he has these barber clippers, so the guy must obviously be pretty good at haircuts, right?

I said, "Doc, we got a little time here. How about giving me a haircut?"

"When do you want it, Goose?" he asked.

"Well," I said. "Here's the terminal, and we got another couple hours. Let's do it in the corner of the terminal here."

"Sure!" he said. "I'd love to give you a haircut!"

So we went over, got a chair, and set up. All the troops

The barber acted like he wasn't listening.
Then I found out he couldn't speak English.

were there, and most of the officers, when he started cuttin' away.

Pretty soon, I saw little smiles. Then I heard a lot of snickers. Then, I heard a lot of *laughter!* And, the worst part about it was that Doc was leading the laughter!

Soon, groups gathered around this haircut. I said, "Doc, I'm startin' to lose confidence in you."

"You'll be alright, Goose!" he said.

Well, before long he was just about down on his knees in laughter. "Doc," I said. "You *have* cut hair before, haven't you?"

He said, "Hell, no! I got these clippers to shave the ass of my four-month-old English bulldog! I've never cut any hair before!"

And that's how Doc got the nickname, "the Butcher." That was on December 28th, and I ain't had a haircut since.

Desert Camo Hat Styles

The desert "chocolate chip" field hat was another item to make its debut in the Gulf. And it faithfully served the troops who wore it, shielding them from the desert sun and undesert-like rains, and often camouflaged their botched up haircuts.

And, true to the wearer's fundamentally American inclination for unconventionality in the face of regimentation, this hat could be bent into a world of fashionable shapes, often caricaturing its distant felt and straw relations.

Standby! Standby!

But not even the flexible desert camo hat could prevail against a *shamal*. What's a shamal? Well, remember in *Lawrence of Arabia*, when "Al Aurens" and the boys were making their way from Aqabah to British Army Headquarters in Cairo, and a deadly sandstorm rolled in? That storm was a shamal.

Every year, scores of these fierce, abrasive "Big Winds" sweep down from the north and rip across the Arabian Peninsula, leaving suffering and mayhem in their wakes. During the Gulf War, our field troops were constantly on alert for a shamal, even a small one, which could disable a piece of equipment, scatter a pallet of supplies, or blow over a shitter in less than a heartbeat.

In fact, one of the most dangerous activities of the Gulf War was trying to land an aircraft during a shamal. But sometimes it had to be done. Then *pride* was involved, as C-130 pilot Capt. Rob "Motorhead" Morecraft explained:

> We flew a C-130 into Ar-ar Base up near the Iraqi border, and we had a sandstorm. Really bad weather, windy. We went in there and tried to find the runway. The navigator guided us in, and we flew right over the runway but couldn't see it.
>
> As soon as the C-141 guys heard that we missed our first pass, they said, if the 130 couldn't land there, there was no way that *they* were gonna be able to get in. They diverted to King Fahd.
>
> But we hooked a 180°, came back around again. The lights which give you your approach angle to the runway told us we were way above the normal glide path. So we decended very rapidly—and landed with about a half mile of visibility in blowing sand.
>
> As we pulled off the runway, the combat control team came up and wanted to shake my hand. They thought it was a great landing. They hadn't seen us till we were on the runway. They said, "Make sure you tell those 141 guys that they don't have a hair on their ass!"

Taking a plane off in "shamal country" could also be something of an adventure. Especially given the peculiar way Saudi air controllers did business, as USAF Maj. Brad Babb remembered:

> At Riyadh, a couple of days ago, a 141 came in and

*Everybody started screaming to get airborne,
but the Saudi controllers couldn't handle it.*

closed down the primary runway with an emergency, so
they had to go to the secondary runway, which, at Riyadh,
is an emergency procedure. And, for the Saudi controllers,
who are highly inflexible, this was a *double* emergency.
There were five or six airplanes stacked up, waiting the
word to take off, and as we sat there, we saw a wall of sand
coming toward us—meaning there was a shamal coming in.

Everybody started screaming, wanting to get airborne
before the sandstorm hit. But the Saudi controller kept
saying, "No one has IFR release yet. No one can be released
into the airspace."

For anything to go abnormal in Saudi airspace is a *big*
emergency for them. They just can't handle it. All those
guys do is say, *"Standby, standby! Abdullah's in the
shitter! He will be back shortly, then you can take off!"*

Christmas in Islam

"Home by Christmas!" was always a rallying cry of earlier wars. But in the Gulf, Christmas came and went before the war had even begun.

The troops celebrated the holiday regardless. Corporal Baldasarre recalled the importance of Christmas to his Marine buddies:

> We had a big Christmas party with near beer, not real beer. In my squad alone, we've got four people who were away from home for the first time, let alone having to do it in a war situation. So it was good to have something to get their minds off home, and try to build up the camaraderie.

One outfit, the Army's 595th Medical Company (Clearing), decided to go all out and make the best of a Christmas far, far from home. But, clearly, this would have to involve considerable improvisation.

For starters, Sgt. David "Heeb" Hebert suggested a tree. Only, there at barren Log Base Charlie, the closest thing to trees were probably rooted in the distant, shifting desert mirages. So, why not improvise one out of something accessible—like sandbags?

"We needed a Christmas tree desperately," Sgt. Michael Malloy explained. "Then Hebert said, 'Well, hey! We don't need any sandbags for the bunker!'"

Indeed, the sandbags weren't doing the bunker much good. Constructed out of plywood and string, it was less than useless— probably dangerous. Malloy continued:

> It was really ingenious, because I don't think there was anybody in Saudi Arabia or in the history of the U.S. Army that ever made a Christmas tree out of sandbags before.
>
> And you can imagine all of the Christmas items that people made to put on it. They took a Pringles can, cut out Mr. Pringles' face, put wings on him, and made him the "Mr. Pringles flying angel."
>
> For gifts, they put MREs under the tree, knowing no one would eat them!

Of course, every Christmas has its downside, usually manifesting itself in melancholy recollections of Christmases past, or absent

*For weeks the company had been inundated
with Christmas packages and letters.*

loved ones. The downer for the 595th involved the recent loss of "Mo," a comrade-in-war lost to "friendly" peanut-butter. Malloy told me about Mo.

I had a spiny-tail lizard. He was slow and very lethargic. His name was Mo. He was pretty cool, he smoked—anybody who was cool in Saudi Arabia smoked, even if they didn't smoke.

He liked peanut butter. I'd put a little milk in it, and then I'd shotgun it. He'd just lick his chops.

I killed him. He wouldn't eat, so I started force-feeding peanut butter down his throat with a straw. I guess I fed him too much.

Mo looked at me in his last moment of life, raised his head, opened his eyes halfway, and just dropped to the ground. I guess he had too much peanut butter. I buried Mo under the Christmas tree, which was kind of symbolic.

The Christmas tree, with its decorations, gifts, and Mo, was just the beginning of this truly memorable holiday. But it was enough to get some troops, like Lt. John Butler, reflecting back on other Christmases, long ago:

> I went to bed on Christmas eve remembering my childhood when I used to always bug my parents to let me open up a present the night before. I faded off into sleep...
> ..Next morning I woke up to a blistering sandstorm.

Desert sandstorms don't just kick up sand, they also blow things down—things like field tents. That's just what happened to the 595th early on Christmas morning. Dr. Howard Heidenberg gave this account:

> I generally like to take care of the soldiers by staying up late at night guarding the cherry stove. Just my way of pitching in a little bit. Also, of keeping warm.
>
> It was pretty comfortable. We were all really happy and snug, commenting on how different it was from the night before when we were getting rained on outside a cucvee [the military's version of a GMC Blazer].
>
> Then, at about 2 o'clock in the morning, the shamal started blowin'. I looked around at the tent. One side was shakin'—but the opposite side from where the wind was blowin'. I remember thinking, *Hmm! That's peculiar.*
>
> It began blowing harder and, suddenly, I heard the fuel can fall off the side of the tent. I thought I'd better go out and investigate. As I reached over to pick up the fuel can, I saw Lieutenant Butler's part of the tent collapse on him. I thought, *Hmm! I'll help out my buddy.*
>
> I reached for his corner of the tent. My hand was but a foot away when, just like in the *Wizard of Oz*, the whole tent suddenly lifted up off of the ground and started to blow away.
>
> "There it goes!" hollered Sergeant Beckwith.
>
> Next I heard the stove go down, and saw Sergeant Beckwith, a pretty big guy, sit up and get wasted by the wind. Then, it was like in the three stooges, where a pie is coming at the camera like at your face. That's how the big tent beam was lookin'—and it was going right for my friend, Woodsy.
>
> So picture it all from the outside: instead of looking at a fully set up tent, you're looking at floors and gear and a bunch of people laying on cots. Except for Woodsy, who was totally sucked into the tent liner.
>
> We'd been *shamalled!*

And there, amidst the devastation, was the Christmas tree Sergeant Hebert had improvised—and Mo.

"The sandstorm tore up the Christmas tree," said Malloy, "and there was Mo laying face up on the ground. I had to rebury him. Poor little Mo."

Instead of a fully set up tent, you're looking at floors and gear and a bunch of people lying on cots.

But shamal or no shamal, the holiday celebration—which the 595th dubbed "Christmas in Islam"—continued. For weeks the company had been inundated with Christmas packages and letters, and it was clear that the mess hall was working really hard to get all the food for the Christmas meal together.

In addition, there was the party the 595th threw for its neighbors in an artillery unit. Sergeant Malloy recalled it:

One of the most memorable times of our Christmas was our party for the 75th Field Artillery. We thought we'd

49

throw a bash for those guys. We gave them near beer, all kinds of tasty Saudi Arabian treats—you have no idea what's in them!—and the famous Vienna sausages.

Sergeant Hebert enlightened us with a rendition of "The Twelve Days of Christmas," which he called "The Twelve Days of Exile." The first line went something like this:

> *On the first day of exile*
> *A jar-head gave to me*
> *A camel burger in a plastic bag.*

And it got worse. The funny thing is nobody knew any of it except the first line and the fifth line. They just went:

> *Twelve blah-blah-blah-blah's*
> *Eleven blah-blah-blah-blah's...*

But when it got to *"FIVE MRE-E-Es!"* everyone sang in unison. Seemed to be the only thing *everyone* remembered.

It was quite original. But the funniest part was watching Sergeant Hebert trying to get the guys to sing. He said, "You can't go haywire until we sing our song!" So the guys were overjoyed to sing it.

Then the guys drowned themselves in near beer, thinking that they were going to get drunk. Some were even *acting* drunk, which I found pretty interesting—there must've been a psychological thing behind that.

Operation "Waitin' on the War"

Before the war started, there was a lot of skepticism about whether we were going to actually go to war, or if Saddam was gonna pull his troops out at the last moment. The fifteenth of January deadline was well known, and we'd been waiting for it like a child would wait for Christmas—except it wasn't really like Christmas.

Sgt. Steve A. Phillips
Alpha Co. 3-41, Tiger Brigade

For many troops, the worst part of Desert Shield was the waiting. The "Big Wait" only seemed to magnify their fears and uncertainties.

So, with Christmas behind them and the unrelenting U.N. deadline ahead, small groups of Americans throughout the theater began creating novel new distractions to ease their anxieties—like the "Mother of All Distractions," dreamed up by the 348th Medical Detachment. The 348th was known affectionately as the "Mickey Mouse Club," because Mickey's face embellished the red crosses on their Huey air ambulances—and because they were always out to get laughs.

Their plan? The launching of a UFO invasion of Saudi Arabia! SFC Russell J. Barnes gave me the following play-by-play of the Mickey Mouse Club's version of "War of the Worlds":

A brief history of the Unidentified Flying Objects which terrorized the Dhaman-Dharan area and probably initiated the acts of aggression by Iraq against the United States of America....

The month of December. A cool night. Several soldiers in the White Elephant compound saw strange, unidentified, glowing objects—many of them flying in clusters of four.

One of the UFOs mysteriously began to descend, working its way down to the bottom floor. Then, it began to ascend again up the stairwell, spreading havoc throughout the barracks.

People screamed, "GAS!" and reached for their gas

masks, but didn't know where they were, because they'd never used them before. In his bathroom, our colonel, the compound commander, slipped in the shower on a bar of soap when women went running in there saying we were being invaded.

Our colonel slipped in the shower when women went running in there saying we were being invaded.

The compound guards said that they believed the UFOs' point of origin was on the roof over the floor in which we lived. They also said that the tinfoil dangling from them may have attracted Patriot fire—but if that's the case, I don't know anything about it.

Half of our detachment was up there, launching homemade UFOs built out of dry-cleaning bags and birth-day cake candles, with plastic soda straws for a frame on the bottom. We probably had eight in the air at once, two groups of four, and were just starting on our third group, when the colonel came up and caught us dead in the act.

At this point, Sgt. Jerry McCrudden cut in:

> After the colonel slipped and busted his butt, he ran
> up to the roof to see what was going on. One of our warrant
> officers, Neil Lubasky, was just gettin' ready to launch
> another UFO. The colonel ran out and screamed, "You!
> Don't let that go!"
> Lubasky said, "Okay!"
> "Okay," the colonel demanded, "show me your ID
> card!"
> "Okay," Neil replied. He let the UFO go.
> *Don't let that go!"* cried the colonel.

Then Barnes came back:

> He was quite upset. He told everyone to go to bed. But,
> when we talked to him the following morning, his exact
> words were, "I couldn't sleep last night. I was too damn
> busy laughing!"
> It was the funniest thing he'd seen—nurses goin' nuts,
> and guards going hysterical.

During the launchings, the wind had been such that it pushed
several UFOs over the Dharan Air Base, at about 1000-1500 feet.
They were in a perfect formation but they wouldn't show up as a
radar blip, so the air traffic controllers flipped out.

Meanwhile, a large cargo aircraft was on its final approach. When
it spotted a group of four UFOs hovering over the air base, the C-130
had to divert. Said Barnes:

> We know for a fact that, as the UFOs disappeared into
> the clouds, the pilot called them in.
> The next day we kept looking at our intelligence
> sources. The only thing that we could figure was that six
> Iraqi helicopters had surrendered themselves. We don't
> really want to take credit for it, but, in retrospect, I think
> we were probably the root cause.
> As we were building the UFOs in assembly line pro-
> duction, we called it, "Operation Waitin' on the War." A
> good thirty of us were involved in building them, launching
> them, and terrorizing the port and the air field. It was great
> fun!

The Storm

THE AIR WAR

*The whole war was just
one big light show!*

Lt. Jeff "Herman" Ruth
USS *Ranger*

Cruise Control

There it goes. First missile. There you go. It's started now. Looks like the Wisconsin didn't go first. Looks like we did. It was kinda quick. I'm tellin' ya, I don't know what to think right now. I'm shaking in my boots. I'll be honest with you, I'm not gonna tell ya some hero-worship stuff that ain't true. It's approximately 1:41 AM now, and we just started a war.

> GMG2 Joe "Taz Devil" Palisano
> USS *Foster*
> from a live audio-taped
> letter to his family

Though humor often played a big role in the Gulf deployment, all joking was hushed momentarily on January 17 by the awesome realization that a new generation of Americans was about to go to war.

The war began for the Navy with the launch of a Tomahawk cruise missile from the destroyer, USS *Paul F. Foster*, sailing somewhere in the night waters of the northern Persian Gulf. Shortly before the order to fire came down, *Foster* captain Comdr. Ed Kujat addressed his 380-man crew:

> The next few days will set the course of the world order for decades to come. If we must fight, we will. If we can restore freedom to Kuwait without a fight, we will. But for you and I, the choice is not ours to make.
>
> I urge every crew member on board to stay alert to your duties and your responsibilities. Take care of the details, and be ready.

When it became clear that a cruise launch was imminent, the ship's crew responded with a strong sense of duty—and a considerable mix of doubt and dread:

> In the beginning, we knew we were launching an attack on Iraq, but we didn't really want to. Before we launched there was total silence. Everybody was wondering, "What's gonna happen? If this bird don't go off, and we're up here, will we survive?" It seemed like the whole repair

locker just came together, when we're usually pickin' at each other.

HTFN Steve Wellford

When it came down to one minute, we didn't say anything, thinking to ourselves it *wasn't* going to happen and it might be called off.

GSE1 Joe Petraglia

There was a little time after we'd fired where we had such a rush. Such a high. We thought, "God, what did we just do? We just launched cruise missiles. At people." It was kind of scary.

GS2 Leif Sabo

I said to myself, "I can't believe we're doing this!" I got knots in my stomach.

GSE1 Petraglia

We knew we'd launched the first Tomahawk to be fired in anger at Iraq. We knew we were starting a war. It was emotional. Everybody sat there, jus' lookin' at each other. It was...breathtaking.

DC3 Winston Mack

While some were catching their breath in the face of this truly historical event, others were busily trying to adjust their routines:

Whenever things get kinda funny and hectic, sailors always come straight in and want breakfast. Before they fired the first set of missiles, they came in for breakfast, went back out to fire the missiles, and then suddenly came back in expecting lunch. We did the best we could, but we had to serve them real small meals. Otherwise we couldn't have done it, because it wasn't a thing we *normally* do.

MSC George Randolph

As the hours passed and missile after missile followed the first Tomahawks into Iraq, with no apparent repercussions to the *Foster*, life aboard ship began to carry on as usual—but not without a good deal of reflecting on the night's work:

The first couple of times it was a really big deal, but after that it got almost routine to fire a Tomahawk missile.
It was surprising how, basically, we started a war and then went back to life as normal.
Before we got here, some people were wondering, "Why

are we here? This is really dumb to be doing this. People are going to die because of us." I doubt that it changed all that much when they fired the Tomahawks. It might have a little. Everybody became...well, maybe not more cynical, but their sense of humor seemed to become a lot more biting.

SE2 Clay Lloyd

Personally speaking, I felt sorry for the Iraqis who were dying just as much as I felt sorry for our guys, you know? For one, I didn't want the war to kick off. I was hopin' they could settle things. But seein' that they couldn't—and it may sound bad to say this—I'm glad it wasn't *our* guys that took the punishment.

HTFN Wellford

Scuttlebutt

Once the initial shockwaves of war began to ebb, the joking resurfaced, often as *scuttlebutt:*

How smart is a cruise missile? So smart that, if it gets lost, it can stop and ask for directions.

Did ya hear about the military building in Bagdad that was designated for attack?

The only problem was that the necessary pre-programming for that target was not available in the Tomahawk's smart guidance system. But the abandoned building across the street fit neatly into the missile's crosshairs.

So they dropped leaflets on the suspect building, warning its occupants of its impending destruction—hoping they would move over to the one that *could* be hit!

Into a Hornets' Nest

"We took off at 2 o'clock in the morning. It was awful dark—probably the darkest night ever," said Capt. Kurt "Killer" Anders of the 42nd Electronic Countersurveillance Ravens, as he recalled the first Air War mission for his EF-111 squadron.

"It was a 'dark and stormy night,'" joked electronic warfare officer (EWO), Lt. Col. Damaso Garcia. "The weather had been really good until *that* freaking night. Then we had the worst weather since we'd been in theater. It was very cloudy. It was night. It was hell!"

"Plus, we fly these big pigs of the sky," Anders said, alluding to their EF-111's unofficial nickname, the Aardvark—meaning "mud pig" in Dutch. The plane had no *official* name, but since it flew low and close to the ground and had a big snout, "Aardvark" it was.

"We got everybody together and went up to the north to meet our tanker," Anders continued. "There were about 12 or 18 other F-111s there, though it seemed like a hundred, all on the same tankers as us. I don't know what the hardest part was—finding the tanker, or avoiding everybody else trying to get on it."

According to Garcia, the weather was really bad at the refueling rendezvous. "Everybody was kind of hanging by their teeth.

"The wings of the tanker were full, but we were just sitting behind everybody, waiting. There was a bit of confusion about who was going to refuel next. Nobody was doing anything, so Anders got on the radio and said, 'Well? Is there anybody who's gotta get gas out of this tanker?'"

"We had to fight our way into it," said Anders. "It was worse than a chow line."

"They didn't have quite as good pilots as we did either," Lt. "Hack" Peahrson, another EWO, added with a chuckle. "So we had to do a lot of compensating for the errors that they made."

After fueling up, the Ravens' flight of four proceeded north toward the Kuwaiti border. Then, about 50 miles ahead of them, they saw the night sky light up. "It was like camera flash bulbs goin' off as you approached," Peahrson said. "They were bombs exploding on the horizon."

The mission took them into Bagdad from the east. There were F-4 Wild Weasels and F-111s also heading that direction. The Raven EF-111s were crammed full of electronics, which were designed to screen the other friendly fighters from Iraqi radar, so it couldn't direct radar-guided weaponry at them.

"It was kinda like a 'Klingon cloaking device,'" Anders said.

As the Ravens closed in on Bagdad, they were confronted for the first time by the incongruities of this new air war. One minute, off in the distance, they'd see the guns lacing the night sky with their antiaircraft fire (AAA). The next minute, they'd catch a glimpse of an Iraqi highway, with cars rolling down it as if it were any other night—just ol' Joe Habib heading home from work—only a stone's throw below them.

Anders, for one, soon realized the dangers involved in their low-level approach:

> The stupidest thing we did during the whole war was when we went down to low level.
>
> It was dark. There was a big, black hole down there, and when you were flying your airplane down into it, you couldn't see the ground with your eyes, so you had to trust all the magic stuff that's in your airplane. You pointed your nose down at the ground, and just prayed that everything was gonna work all right and do its thing.

To be effective, the Ravens couldn't fly in a tight formation. They had to string themselves out, one behind another, which, as "Hack" Peahrson found, created more problems:

> My plane was third in formation and, at low level, when the guys out ahead went through, they would kick up a hornets' nest. So when we came through, all the triple-A came shooting up over the top of us—tracers and orange flashes.

The pilots were talking it up on their radios, helping one another avoid the AAA as it blazed away at them. Every time one of those big guns fired, it lit up the cockpit like broad daylight.

"It was the *first* enemy fire we came across," recalled Garcia, "and I remember thinking, *'Hell! They're trying to kill us!'*"

Maj. Larry "Spitz" Spitzer, driver for EWO Peahrson, tried his best to sit back in formation and dodge the AAA bursts:

> Hack was over on the right hand side having problems with the electronic warfare crap. We had a radar and a TFR [terrain following radar] scope, both of which are required to fly safely. The radar was giving me nothing, just a couple of lines strobing across it, so I yelled, "Hey, Hack. How about the radar?"

"Yeah, yeah, yeah," he said. "I'm trying." Finally, he screamed, *"Shit!* Everything quit over here. The whole damn thing quit!"

And I went, "Can you get anything out of this machine or not?"

"Yeah! Yeah! I can work it! But I'm gonna have to get inside it. And you're gonna have to take the navigation."

"Oh great!" I yelled. "If you can't get anything out of that system, we're getting the hell out of here, because shit's going up everywhere and I'll be damned if we're going up here for nothing!"

"No, no! I can do it," he said. "I'm workin' on it. You just go, and I can get it all worked out."

So I did. This guy had some *big balls,* but he was just a lieutenant and I'd be goddamned if he was gonna make *me* look bad. I was pressin' on!

So we went along at about 1000 feet, and I saw a big streak of light as a missile was launched. Turns out it was about 30 miles away, probably shootin' at somebody over Bagdad, but it sure as *shit* looked like it was comin' at *us!*

I screamed, *"Give me four hundred foot on the TFR!"* If we could get lower, we could get away from it. So he says, "Uh, okay," reaches over, gives me 400 foot, and goes back to workin' on his system.

So there we were—flying at 400 foot TFR, the most dangerous thing we'd done all night. We couldn't see a god-dang thing. The systems and monitors wouldn't tell us what was going on. We were just trusting in our airplane and God. And the missile blows up. About 30 miles away.

The mission's plan to exit from Iraq required a synchronized turn by the four Ravens at an airspeed of 510 knots, which would have resulted in a close formation for the flight home. But Major Spitzer had other plans:

As all the shit was going on, I had the thing *cobbed.* I don't know how fast we were going, but we figured that, since we were the first ones out of there, the other guys would be so far behind us that we'd be back at home station by the time they crossed the border.

So we went up, made the turn—and a generator dropped off-line. The plane did all kinds of weird things. I was thinking, Geezus christ. What more could happen? The hell with all this!

Hack sat back, calm, cool, and collected. If he'd had a cigarette, he probably would've taken a puff. "How's it going?" he asked.

"Shitty!" I said. "We're gettin' out of here!"

So we left as fast as the damn thing would go. And when we got near the border, we checked with the AWACs to see how far we were from the number four plane. He was supposed to be somewhere behind us—way behind us!

Cars rolled down the highway, only a stone's throw below the EF-111s.

Well, we got the reading and couldn't figure it out. Nothing was matching up.

As it turns out, all of us had had the same damn idea. We turned our lights back on and I realized my old buddy Anders was *ahead* of me. We were both going out of there like scalded-ass apes!

As he neared home, Captain Anders tuned his radio to the BBC. There was no news yet indicating that the war had started. He heard stories on the futures market and Wall Street and things happening all around the globe, but they weren't even covering the Gulf.

"It was kinda neat," Anders reflected, "because we were there and back before the world even knew about it."

As they landed back home, all safe and reasonably sound, the four Raven crews were greeted by Sgt. Darren Krackow, their life-support man. It was his job to take care of all the personal flight equipment, from radios to breathing gear. And nobody was happier to see the first mission end:

> You get to know these guys after awhile. So when they go out and fly, in the back of your head you get to wondering if, God forbid, they won't come back. It's a terrible feeling, thinking about it.
>
> But the first night, when everybody came back, it was tremendous! Seeing them all walk in, listening to the stories they had. They were psyched up, and, since I was the first person they really saw, everybody just started spillin' their guts. And they all had ten pillow packs (urine bags) filled up—it was such a *long* mission!

The Ravens learned quickly from their first encounter with the Iraqis. They didn't need to get in so close. After that they held it at a higher altitude. "It wasn't quite so scary the next night," said Spitzer.

BBC SPECIAL REPORT

War has begun in the Gulf. Tonight Allied forces, including British, Saudi Arabian, and Kuwaiti fighter bombers, have launched full attacks on Iraq and Kuwait. The first attacks began around midnight Greenwich mean time, preceded by a wave of cruise missiles launched from warships.

American officials say there were four hundred raids in the first three hours on sixty separate targets. First reports from the Allied side suggest that the Iraqi Air Force has been devastated. The signal plotting official says all those involved in the initial attacks returned safely, and the attacks have been more successful than could be imagined...

Received aboard the USS *Foster*

"This war is real!"

In their ready room aboard the USS *Ranger*, the aviators of Intruder squadron VA-155 waited for a weather briefing. There were at least 40 guys packed into the room. Everyone wore a new sanitized flight suit. They just sat there, quiet and introspective, staring at each other, with no real idea of what it would be like out there. Or if they would go out at all.

Then the admiral walked in.

"I know all of you are in here briefing," he said, "wondering whether or not you're gonna go. Well, I just want to be the one to tell you that, right now, there's a hundred and twenty cruise missiles headed into Bagdad."

The hush that fell over the room was deafening. Then he said something that no one quite comprehended at the time—they were all too scared to get it.

"I really envy you guys," he said. "You get to go fight it."

But once they did get out there and "fight it," most realized that the admiral had been right. It was probably the most exciting thing that any of them had ever known.

As one of the A-6 guys told me later: "I wouldn't have traded it for anything in the world!"

While the admiral was down below giving his ready room talk to VA-155, two Tomcats from fighter squadron VF-2 prowled on CAP (Combat Air Patrol) high above the *Ranger*. The F-14s had launched at midnight. It was now just after 1:30 AM. Lt. Comdr. Mike "Spanky" Gennette, who piloted one of the planes, remembered vividly his first indications that the war had begun:

> We started seeing what we thought were flares coming out of the ships on the water. We didn't know exactly what they were at that point. It turned out we were seeing a bunch of Tomahawk launches.
>
> Then we saw a multitude of aircraft with high altitude coming from the U.A.E. (United Arab Emirates), which turned out to be squadrons of F-16s on their way to the initial strike missions up in the north Gulf.

Lt. Comdr. Robert "Herb" Wilson, an RIO (Radar Intercept Officer)

Guys would launch, and thirty minutes later
Peter Arnett would be saying, "Holy shit!"

aboard a VF-1 Tomcat, also caught the first action of the war from on high:

> Everyone was anticipatin' the first attack, from the time the Jan. 15 deadline was over. We were all wondering, "When's it gonna start? When's it gonna start?"
>
> The morning of January 17th, we were out flying when the shipboard controller radioed us and said, "If you look down and to your left, you're going to see 32 T-LAMS (Tomahawks) in-bound." Our wingman picked them up on the radar and about fifteen seconds later we saw lights in northern Kuwait explode like the Fourth of July. I thought, *Well, I guess we're not just shittin' around anymore!*

Soon more F-14s were launched to relieve those already on CAP. Among the next guys out was Lt. "Ollie" Olivarez. Herb recalled how he and Ollie had worked out a system to pass on the latest war news:

I told him before I took off, "If the war starts, I'll give you a call sign when you guys come out." Since Ollie was of Hispanic descent, the code word chosen was SALSA. And sure enough, there *was* a war and SALSA was used.

About this time, a helo from the USS *Foster* was patrolling in the same vicinity with its radio tuned to CNN. The pilot, Lt. James White, thought it humorous that the reporters in Bagdad couldn't distinguish between Tomahawk missiles and bombers.

They said, "Gee, there's bombs going off everywhere, but we can't see any planes—they must *really* be fast!" It was funny because *we* knew what was going on—the missiles were going in.

Meanwhile, back aboard the *Ranger*, down in the bowels of the ship where no aviator dares to tread, Bosun's Mate Walter McNairy relaxed on his bunk:

I was laying on my rack when the captain came over the horn and said, "Well, fellas, the Air Force has launched its first attack. We're going to launch ours at about four o'clock."
I sat up in my rack thinking, *All right! This war is real!*

By this time, Spanky Gennette had landed back on the carrier. He went into the chow hall, ate a "slider" (hot dog), and watched Bernard Shaw and Peter Arnett getting bombed in Bagdad. Nearby, another aviator was chuckling over the CNN reports:

Guys would launch from the *Ranger* on a strike, and about 30 minutes later Peter Arnett would be live from Bagdad saying, "Holy shit! Look what's coming in!" And everyone back on the *Ranger* was watching and cheering!

Attack from the "Bat Caves"

The bombers, fighters and Tomahawk cruise missiles snared the headlines on Operation Desert Storm's first day. But the first shots fired in anger were unleashed by Army AH-64 Apache helicopters.

At precisely 2:38 a.m. on Jan. 17, laser-guided Hellfire missiles began bursting into two early-warning control intercept sites in far western Iraq. Within four minutes, both were completely destroyed.

The mission was an unqualified success. "Expect No Mercy" is the battalion's motto, and in this first air combat action of the war, the promise did not go unfulfilled.

SSgt. William H. McMichael
SOLDIERS magazine

This daring mission marked the "baptism by fire" for the Apache helicopter, and its success dispelled all remaining doubts about the reliability and effectiveness of one of America's latest high-tech weapons. It also brought the press flocking in and made instant heroes of Lt. Col. Dick Cody and his men.

However, while the raid itself hit the news, there was another *untold* story behind the published accounts that made the mission's success all the more remarkable. It was the story of crew endurance, and the difficulty the 1st Battalion had in maintaining it.

When told early on they'd be going to an air base in Saudi Arabia, naturally the Apache crews assumed, at the very least, they'd have a place to sleep, good ground transportation, and a suitable area to park their helos. But it didn't quite turn out that way. A parking garage served as living quarters, salvaged vehicles as transport, and a hotly disputed airport ramp as parking for the aircraft. Still, the 1st Battalion adapted to these shortcomings and got on with its job.

Another inadequacy, however, presented a tougher nut to crack, as WO1 Jerry Orsbern recalled:

We were trying to maintain a posture for anything, because we didn't know what was happening. The news flow initially was very slow. And since we didn't have any radios, we couldn't even pick up BBC.

We ended up having one company on "REDCON 4" for night operations, so it could launch at any hour. But that became a problem, because from August to October it was *extremely* hot over here. These night crews were supposed to be resting in the daytime, but it was so hot they couldn't get to sleep.

They flew a fifteen-million-dollar aircraft,
but were hanging out in the "Bat Caves."

Obviously, what 1st Battalion needed was some *cool* space during the day—only, given the base pecking order, that kind of space was in short supply for the Apache crews. Cody finally found the solution in a place no one else had even considered:

The King Fahd Airport complex was so huge that it had these big ducts, two or three miles' worth of tunnel space, that ran underneath the runways to house all their wiring. They were the coolest spot in town. And that's where my night crews slept—down there like bats. They flew a fifteen-million-dollar aircraft, but were hanging out in the "Bat Caves."

So it was, thanks in no small part to the "Bat Caves" and the crew endurance they provided, that the first mission of Desert Storm succeeded. And how successful was it?

Well, the attack went off *precisely* on schedule; the bomb damage assessment (BDA) showed *all* targets were destroyed; *no* injuries were sustained by the crews and *none* of their equipment was damaged or lost; and all of this was accomplished under severe environmental circumstances. That's pretty successful by anybody's standards.

But the outbreak of hostilities brought new challenges for Colonel Cody, the biggest of which was keeping his people in fighting trim, as a mean, lean, disciplined team. After all, back then no one knew how long the war would last. And the colonel was determined not to lose a single man through sloppy judgement or poor procedures.

Cody proved himself more than equal to the task. He drove his crews mercilessly. And, though they often griped about the strict regimen, Cody never came close to losing any of them—*except once*, in the face of a threat even he had not anticipated:

> We had a crew chief spend four days at the Fleet Hospital, and he came back with a Navy nurse's panties. He was bragging about it for quite some time. I was really afraid we might have a lot of self-inflicted wounds after that.

"Sir, guess what?"

When, once an hour, Army Sgt. Steve Phillips of the Tiger Brigade's 3rd Battalion, 41st Infantry, announced over his company's radio net, "News rep as follows," everyone dropped what they were doing and listened up.

Phillips had the only radio in Alpha Company tuned to AFN, the Armed Forces Network, so he would pick up the latest news broadcasts and relay them to his fellow troops over their tactical sets. Maybe it was secondhand news—but the troops still listened intently. They knew the war would kick off any day, and when it did, their "Tiger Tough" unit was sure to play a big part.

As the U.N. deadline crept closer, the men of Alpha Company became increasingly enthralled by Phillips' reports. Sometimes they'd hear about troops moving north. "And we'd go like, 'Wow! We might be moving out!'" recalled Sergeant Hamilton "Oakie" Rigney.

Then the fifteenth of January passed, and still the Iraqis weren't backing down. Everyone expected war at any moment. But, when it happened, no one expected to hear it from Sergeant Phillips. Surely *that* news would come in a briefing by the company commander himself.

The sixteenth came and went. Still, nothing.

Then, on the morning of the seventeenth, Alpha Company got the word. They would move north that morning, up toward the Kuwaiti border. This movement had been in the works for several days, so it came as no surprise. But as the soldiers were awakened at the predetermined time, Sergeant Phillips came over the radio. "I got a news report. Anyone interested?"

"Send it! Send it!" everyone hollered.

"The United States has just started bombing Iraqi forces," he reported.

Rigney, still half asleep, muttered to himself, "That can't be true! We would know before it came out on the news!"

Soon, the others were saying the same thing—"It can't be real! The lieutenant would know first!"

Then the lieutenant came on the radio. "Phillips, are you serious or are you bullshittin'?"

"I'm serious!" answered Phillips.

"Well, there ain't anybody told me about this!" the lieutenant yelled.

71

Then AFN announced it was initiating 24-hour live coverage—"Desert Storm: The War in the Gulf," they called it. So, Sergeant Phillips began giving the troops a steady play-by-play on the news as he got it from AFN. He gave accounts of bombing sorties over Kuwait, cruise-missile strikes on Bagdad, B-52 raids against the Republican Guard.

Everyone expected war at any moment, but no one expected to hear it from Sergeant Phillips.

And, while the sergeant continued his reporting to the troops, the lieutenant reported to the company CO.

"*Sir, guess what!*" he said.

"We were in the Army, and we were supposed to be the first ones to know," Rigney told me later, chuckling. "Yet there we were, actually in a state of war, and the people back home knew about it before we did. I thought that was quite ironic."

The Light Show

We saw the B-52 raids come in and watched them light up the ground. Next thing, we looked down and the ground was shootin' at us. It was real quiet, but there was this amazing light show going on. Then the Prowlers shot their HARM (High-speed Anti-Radiation) missiles. We saw a big ol' flash of light when a missile came off their airplanes. The whole war was just this one big light show!

Lt. Jeff "Herman" Ruth
USS *Ranger*

Every night-flying pilot I visited with in the Gulf was absolutely awestruck by the war's dazzling light displays. Not surprising, I suppose, when you consider that most of these flyers were young men who had seen nothing more spectacular before than a hometown Fourth of July finale.

But even the veterans, like Comdr. Bug Roach, were genuinely impressed. "It was like watching the Disneyland fireworks from one of the skyrockets!" he said.

Navy Lt. Kelly "Booger" Barager's favorite "fun" attraction was when the battleships fired their big guns:

> I watched the battleships doin' their business. That was beautiful. They were launching their big ol' VWs, Toyotas and Subarus. You'd just sit there and smile, and a couple minutes later they'd launch some more. It was really pretty.

As the light spectacles continued to unfold, the enthralled flyers remained alert—at least subconsciously—to the fact that this was all happening during a war. And often a guy's built-in reflexes would suddenly override his appreciation of the "pretty" lights around him and jar him back into the reality that people were still trying to kill him.

One night, so much stuff was lighting up the sky that the pilot of an E-2 Hawkeye began screaming over the radio, "We're being shot at! We're being shot at!"

"We're going lower," the guy hollered.

Spanky Gennette, who was flying CAP near the E-2, hollered back, "No, don't do that! Don't go down! Just keep moving the airplane!"

Actually, what the E-2 pilot saw was just the USS *Wisconsin* firing Tomahawks into Iraq.

Sometimes it was the light from *inside* a cockpit that rudely interrupted things. Lt. Tom "Pickle" Vlasic of the VA-145 Swordsmen, remembered a few times when he tried to take pictures from his Bombardier-Navigator (BN) seat in an A-6. Every time the camera flash went off, the wingman jinked. "I don't know what his problem was," Vlasic chuckled.

But it wasn't just all of those man-made lights that triggered cockpit confusion, as EF-111 pilot, Capt. Jeff "Bake" Baker, discovered:

> Late the first night, we were heading north across the border. I was number two ship in the formation. Suddenly I saw this bright streak across the sky, and my electronic warfare officer yelled, "Holy shit!"
>
> We started doing our best defensive reactions against this unknown entity in front of us. We kept punching out chaff and flares. When our hearts finally settled down a little, we realized we had been defending against a shooting star.

Something equally startling happened to Navy Lt. Chris "Quiver" Burgess. One night, as he cruised along at 25,000 feet, suddenly Venus popped out from behind the clouds:

> The guy in the back seat thought it was a SAM missile and was yelling, "Break left! Break left!"
>
> I looked over for a second and kinda stared at it, then said, "Hey, Jay, I think that's a star..."
>
> Jay was pretty quiet for the rest of the flight after that.

After this incident, nobody in Burgess' VAQ-131 Lancer squadron wanted to say he saw *anything*, for fear of suffering a similar humiliation. As a result, it got pretty hairy at times—like when a pilot stared down at an oil well fire and swore, momentarily, it was a SAM coming up to get him.

But, of all the Gulf War's light displays, the most dramatic may have been the one that featured an *absence* of light. Another VF-2 Bounty Hunter, Lt. Comdr. Ed "Shoebo" Daniels, explained:

> The best light show I saw was when we were up at Whiskey 9, a combat air patrol station ten miles off the

*Night-flying pilots were absolutely awestruck
by the war's dazzling light displays.*

Kuwaiti coast. We'd been there a couple of hours when suddenly a bomb went in and we saw it go off. That meant we still had airplanes up there. Fine.

Then another went in and we saw—not just the bomb going off—but a big *arcing* light. About three seconds later, the entire Kuwaiti coastline went black. Seventy miles of coastline, and they'd just taken out its main transformer!

It was a beautiful, shit-hot thing!

Cleared for Takeoff

If the light shows provided an *up side* for many pilots in the Air War, the *down side* was the frustrating tendency of Iraqi airmen to run rather than fight. Comdr. Bug Roach elaborated on it:

> The fighter guys were pretty disappointed that the Iraqi Air Force chose not to come up. The fighters did their job *too* well, because the fighters' reputation kept the Iraqis at bay. They never launched. They ran before us, so to speak. It surprised everybody, I think, because they had the fourth largest Air Force in the world. We were anticipating a major air battle. But, as things turned out, their Air Force took leave the day the war began, sitting around in Iran on R'n'R—which probably didn't encourage their ground troops, who were sitting there getting the shit kicked out of them.

Even when, on rare occasions, the Iraqis *did* vector their planes at ours, all our pilots had to do was turn their "pointy ends" towards them, and Saddam's boys would skeedaddle—leaving the Americans unchallenged and incredibly frustrated.

Apparently the frustration was just too much for a couple of Marine flyers. When these Harrier guys made an attack on the Al Jaber Air Base in Kuwait, they couldn't resist bombing the closest thing they'd seen yet to an enemy aircraft—a static display, a "plane-on-a-stick" mounted at the entrance to the airfield.

But these marines must have flown away more frustrated than ever. While they left bomb craters all around the symbolic target, the plane itself remained untouched.

It occurs to me that this all may seem pretty absurd if you don't savvy a character trait unique to the fighter pilot. In a nutshell, I guess I'm talking "attitude." An attitude rooted in a fierce, competitive spirit. An attitude that defines success, not in terms of actual injuries inflicted, but of challenges met; one that defines disappointment, not in terms of opponents escaped, but of battles unjoined. Maybe the best way to illustrate this, in the context of the Gulf War, is to take you along on a typical Gulf War fighter mission. This time your pilot is Comdr. Dave Bernard—call sign, "Barnyard":

> A fighter pilot's dream, without a doubt, is to engage the enemy, successfully defeat him in an air-to-air arena,

BAGHDAD AIR SHOW 1991

COME SEE THE LATEST IN AVIATION TECHNOLOGY

FEATURING AERIAL DEMONSTRATIONS OF THE:

F-15	F-16	A-10	AWACS	B-52
F-111	F-14	F-18	AV-8	A-4
F-117	AC-130	JUGAR	TORNADO	F-1

FIREPOWER DEMONSTRATIONS EVERY HALF HOUR

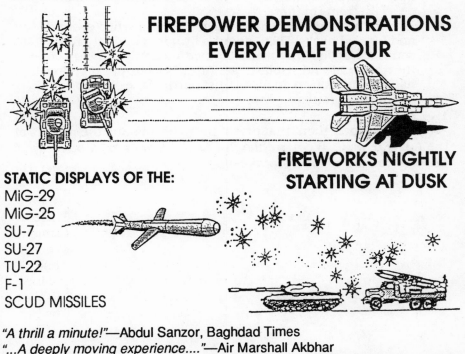

FIREWORKS NIGHTLY STARTING AT DUSK

STATIC DISPLAYS OF THE:
MiG-29
MiG-25
SU-7
SU-27
TU-22
F-1
SCUD MISSILES

"A thrill a minute!"—Abdul Sanzor, Baghdad Times
"...A deeply moving experience...."—Air Marshall Akbhar
"Saddam, how do you like our thousand points of light so far?"—George Bush

watch him go down in flames, and then go back to the home base and paint a little flag of the enemy country on the side of your jet.

And it was always tucked in the back of my mind that there were still some of those Iraqis flying around out there, and I thought, *One of those guys may just be stupid enough to get airborne.*

On our first mission over the beach, we picked a contact right at the end of the hop. There was a lot of haze and it was really hard to see, but we went chargin' down in. Everything looked good. I was thinking, *Oh boy, this is a bad guy—I'm gonna blow him away!*

And what did we see, but a couple of helicopters arcing along the river. Not fair game. Can't touch them.

So we went up for one more hop over the beach. Okay, I thought, *This is my last chance. I'll show these guys!*

We flew all the way to Bagdad. I couldn't believe it. Even over the international airport, there wasn't a plane in sight. It looked like Tumbleweed City. It's amazing to see a place that big with no activity whatsoever.

Actually, Bagdad looked beautiful from 25,000 feet. A pretty city, a lot of farming between the Tigris and Euphrates, and the river snaking through. It looked really calm and peaceful from up there.

So, nothing happened. No activity. I turned around and headed back. Then, about a hundred and fifty miles south of Bagdad, an American voice suddenly came up on the radio and said, "Splash one Fitter!" Some Air Force guy had just shot down an SU-20 just north of the city, and we had just been there.

Small wonder, then, that one of the jokes making the rounds of the Air War was: *What are the five words feared most by an Iraqi pilot?—"You are cleared for take-off!"*

Desert Moon

The war began with a bang for SSgt. Rick Torres, of the Marine Harrier squadron, VMA-311 Tomcats—or, actually, with *two* bangs. Make that two *booms*.

Torres worked the night shift in aircraft maintenance. The Harriers would fly during the day and, at night, Torres and the rest of the "Powerline" crew would service them and make repairs.

The night after Desert Storm began, the Tomcats remained on full alert at King Aziz Naval Air Base. Like their brothers-in-arms elsewhere in the theater, many of these guys were convinced that the highly touted Iraqi military machine would respond to coalition attacks with massive counterblows. Sure as hell, *anything* could happen at *anytime*.

"Late that night, the guys were walking around, towing airplanes and working on top of them," Torres recalled, "when, suddenly, we heard—*BOOM! BOOM!*—and we thought, *Holy shit! The war is here! They're coming in on us!*

"People were running everywhere, putting on gas masks and chemical suits, and ducking for cover. Everybody just went *crazy*."

But, as it turned out, the marines had only experienced sonic booms from two low-flying British Tornados. Still, it showed just how primed the Tomcats were for *something* serious to happen—a fact not lost on Gunny Anthony "Chef" Santo, the next victim of a bogus attack.

It seems that one of the 311th's staff sergeants was a "worst-case scenario" type of guy. The "Grim Reaper," the other Tomcats called him, because of his tendency to promote all the gloom and doom projections. According to Gunny Santo, "He thrived on the idea of four thousand Iraqis in the foxhole with you.

"Then one night he told us two divisions could be rolling down south and be at our positions by the next morning."

While most of the Tomcats pretty much ignored the guy, others—like Santo—couldn't shake the Reaper's cataclysmic forecasts:

> Sure enough, first thing the next morning I heard weapons going off. I thought World War III was coming at me. I jumped up and ran out of the tent to find out what was going on. I was the only one, though, who seemed to be interested. I couldn't understand it. I hollered, *"What was that?"*

*While most ignored the cataclysmic forecasts,
others couldn't shake them.*

And somebody answered, "Oh, they're just practicing over there at the firing range."

Even the pilots, those usually carefree, fly-by-the-seat-of-your-britches Harrier jocks, were affected by the high-seriousness of the situation. This was particularly true the day the war kicked off. SSgt. Rob Finnegan remembered watching them as they came out onto the flight line to launch.

"They knew they were going out for the first time to drop bombs for real. Everybody had *really* serious looks on their faces."

Too serious, figured the Powerline guys, who proceeded to lighten things up. "Just tryin' to have a little bit of fun in a serious situation, is what it boiled down to," said SSgt. T.R. Graham, as he described how 25 of the maintenance crew lined the runway and *mooned* the Harriers as they took off.

Go for a Stuckey's

The joke was that if you couldn't find a target, you'd go bomb a Stuckey's, because if you blow up their Stuckey's or their International House of Pancakes, you kill the nation's will to live.

I don't know if we ever actually did that, but if we didn't know what we hit, we'd always come back and say, "Oh, man! You should have seen that sign go! There were Stuckey's signs everywhere! It was great!"

Lt. Ken Stefanek
69th TFS Werewolves

During the Air War, the flyers who bombed the Iraqi "will to live" into smithereens were showered with many well-deserved kudos. But what of the Intelligence people (INTEL) responsible for plotting those daily missions that won the pilots their glory? Unfortunately, INTEL received little if any credit for their efforts. That is, except when things went wrong. Then they got *all* the credit they could handle, usually in the form of some good-natured ribbing from the air crews.

So, when a pilot returned from a mission where the pre-selected target hadn't quite panned out, he'd utter a quip to the INTEL guys like, "We bombed some very accurately plotted, 3-digit coordinate sand dunes!"

More often than not, Intelligence did the best job it could. Failures in targeting were more a matter of Iraqi cleverness than of INTEL incompetence. But, on the other hand, sometimes there *were* huge discrepancies between what an INTEL officer perceived and what the pilots found to be true.

For instance, there was the case of the fifteen disappearing trucks. "Flat Top" Todd explained:

Some of the targeting was strange. Once they sent two F-16s out against a group of fifteen trucks. Then for two weeks in a row, AWACS kept saying, "Yeah, there's a group of fifteen trucks!" and they'd give us the coordinates. And we'd go out looking for 'em—but no luck. It must've been one group of trucks that the Iraqis moved all around!

*INTEL received little if any credit for their efforts,
except when things went wrong.*

Another Werewolf joked that maybe the Iraqis themselves had developed some stealth capability—the *Stealth Truck!*

But, far and away, the best targeting screw-up story I heard was another by "Flat Top":

> I don't know if this is funny or sad, but the first few days of the war they had all those briefings up at Riyadh. One time Schwarzkopf was out there saying how great all the smart bombs were—how they were "smarter than your average Iraqi." And then he goes, "This is my counterpart's headquarters in Bagdad. You see that building there?" And then suddenly a bomb goes flying into it and— *BOOM!*—the doors all blow off. I thought, *That was a good INTEL source!*
>
> The very next morning, I was woke up at 3 o'clock. I went in to brief and found myself looking at this building in downtown Bagdad which was to be my target for the day.

It was that *same* building. I sat there and said, "I saw this last night on TV! It's blown up! There's nothing in there, believe me!"

Bad weather cancelled the mission, but, four days later, when the targeting came out again, it was that *exact same building!* Later I was up there flying a CAP mission over Bagdad, looked down, and there was a hole in the roof of that building where a bomb had gone through, and the walls were all blown down. I couldn't understand why, in the war, I was targeted twice against that same destroyed building!

Greatest Hits

The biggest thing that me and "Elvis" talked about on every single mission was our main objective, BOPAH— Bring Our Pink Asses Home.

Capt. James "Chainsaw" McCullough
335th Tactical Fighter Squadron Chiefs

If you had asked the flyers of any squadron in the Gulf Theater for their *primary* mission in Desert Storm, I'll bet to a man they would have said "BOPAH."

But, if you'd asked them for their *second* most important reason for being there, differing opinions would have appeared like arseholes— cuz everybody had one. One guy was fighting to free Kuwait. Another was protecting America's energy interests. Still another was ridding the world of Saddam. And so on and so forth.

Only in one unit, the Eagle drivers of the 335th TFS, did I find any sort of consensus on the second purpose for waging this war. And the reason behind their consensus?—*video!* These guys were blessed with great combat video potential.

Pilots are glory guys by nature, but when the Chiefs discovered all the possibilities crammed in a few feet of video tape, video production quickly became a very *high* priority mission. Officially, the footage was for BDA (battle damage assessment), since the video shots allowed the pilots instant BDA. Unofficially, it was for CNN.

And the Chiefs made a *lot* for CNN. Some of the fellas saw the importance of this coverage in helping to keep up morale on the homefront. Said Capt. Chris Hill, "Our laser-guided targeting-pod video did pretty well on TV, encouraging the folks back home with our progress here."

Others saw great PR opportunities in the video. "After all, you can't forget the folks who pay the bills," another Chief said. "No bucks, no Buck Rogers."

But the best part of flying "CNN-capable," and the *real* reason it rated such a high priority with the 335th, was that it was so *personally* gratifying for the pilots. In the past, only the INTEL types were privy to the Chiefs' talented bombing, whereas now, suddenly, the *whole world* was watching.

As I visited with the Chiefs in their ready room at Al Kharj, I could see how genuinely thrilled they were with their video efforts. So thrilled, indeed, that they put together a collection of the squadron's favorite shots, which they dubbed, "Greatest Hits."

Many of these shots never made it to TV, at least in their "Greatest Hits" form. These were the *real* takes, and included a lot of stuff that

The Eagle drivers of the 335th were blessed with great combat video potential.

the powers-that-be back home must have figured was just too "graphic" to broadcast.

For instance, in the 335th's collection you actually see people moving around on the ground—often, not just moving, but *running* for their lives. As I watched the "Greatest Hits" tape, Capt. Tim "TB" Bennett explained how the infrared images of people changed in correlation with their rising body temperatures:

In the target IR (infrared) the more a guy runs, the *whiter* he gets. A couple of times we saw trucks jack-knifed on the road, and we'd take a look at them through the scope. The guys would run away from the trucks, come back, run away, come back, and the more they ran, the hotter—and whiter—they got.

Sure enough, as Bennett talked, I could see the Iraqis on the squadron monitor, running for cover and getting whiter by the second. No, I hadn't seen *that* on CNN.

Then I switched my focus to the audio, concentrating on the flyers' radio lingo as they homed in on a communications tower. Bombardier Capt. Larry Bowers' driver keyed up the mike first:

Pilot:
Just aim for the far base of the tower.

Bowers:
Let's pickle it. Okay...bombs away. And it's a long fly ball! Looks like it's headed for the tower! He's dropping back! Roll out.

Pilot:
Roger.

Bowers:
Fifteen seconds. Will he get it? Will he get it? Looks like he may get it!

Pilot:
Oh, shit. Look at it goin'! Look at it goin', Larry!

Bowers:
You almost can't steer the goddamn laser!—*Shackimundo!*

Pilot:
Holy fucking great!

I remember thinking to myself, *If that piece made it to CNN, they must have bleeped it!* But the serious bleeping was yet to come. Back to Captain Bowers:

They were tagged to go up and hit a radar site using LGBs (Laser Guided Bombs). However, Chuck's backseater wasn't pod qualified, so they threw *me* in with Chuck instead. Chuck is a real intelligent person, but he gets excited very easy.

We went in and dropped our bombs on the radar site. When you hit radars, sometimes you'll hit gas tanks and such, but the secondary explosions really wouldn't be that great. So we always saved a couple of bombs for their ammo storage bunkers.

We rolled in, dropped our first bomb on one of those bunkers, and when we hit it, it was just like the Fourth of July goin' off! There was stuff like missiles going up to *our* altitude—and we were at twenty thousand feet! It was just a *massive* explosion.

As we rolled back in, these missiles started flying in front of the airplane, and Chuck started getting extremely excited. All you could hear was, "Oh fuck! Look at that shit! Goddammit!"

He's very excitable, but I'm not. I just take things in stride. And there we were going down the chute, and it was all I could do to try and calm him down so we could get another bomb off.

At this point, "Chainsaw" McCullough cut in to finish the tale, describing the final scene of Bowers' "Greatest Hits":

So Larry and Chuck are going away from the target, and they're ten or fifteen miles away from it but you can still see missiles shooting out of it, and it's glowing bigger than shit. And you hear Chuck goin', *"Oh, Larry! Look at it, Larry! Look at it burn, Larry!"* He sounds like he's having an orgasm or something. It's pretty unbelievable.

But the most exciting thing to come out of Larry's mouth is, "Not a bad night's work, Chuck!"

Claims to Fame

Deny everything, admit nothing, and make false counter accusations.

The Pilot's Creed

Every war has its own remarkable achievements. Desert Storm was no different. Among its battlefield claims to fame were the first Apache helo attack, the first Tomahawk missile launch, the first Patriot/SCUD encounter, the first M1-A1 tank engagement, and, of course, the first combat use of MREs.

But these were milestones of the "major" variety. The Gulf War also had its share of less heralded, minor events—insignificant, perhaps, in light of the big picture, but memorable indeed to the troops who participated in them.

For the sake of illustrating this point, let's select a typical bunch of troops—say, a squadron of flyers, like the Silver Foxes of VA-155. And let's start with their CO, Comdr. J. P. F. "Just Plain Frank" Sweigert, who happened to lead the war's very first carrier strike "over the beach" on January 17th. Surely, Sweigert and his family and friends will never forget that one.

Then there was Lt. Dan "Snake" Kalal. "Snake" doubled as the squadron's senior landing signal officer—meaning, it was *he* who had to lecture the Silver Foxes on the importance of correct carrier landings, which led to his memorable first:

> As a senior LSO up on the platform, I was giving a lecture just prior to the start of one of our line periods. The biggest thing we were working on was our boarding rate— how *not* to bolter (make a bad landing approach).
>
> After chewing everybody else out for having terrible boarding rates, I ended up being the *first* to bolter.
>
> Actually, I was just trying to ease some of the tension off of everyone else.

And there was the squadron executive officer, Comdr. Larry Munns, who performed what his shipmates claimed was the war's first "close air support" by an A-6 Intruder:

> Supposedly, it was to be a normal catapult shot off of

CAT 3. We launched in an airplane with five tanks on it.
In all, they had 10,000 lbs. of fuel, or 1400 gallons, which
was more gas than you'd burn in your car in your lifetime.

When you hit the end of the catapult, you always feel
a smack. But as soon as we were off the deck, we felt this

**Apparently, somebody went in and bombed the hell
out of this restaurant that looked like a ship.**

other bump. I glanced over at Ploofer and asked him, "Is
anything wrong over there?"

Just then someone called us on our radio and said,
"Four-one-two, looks like you're missing a drop tank."

Ploofer looked out his window and said, "I'm missing a
couple over here. How you doing on your side?"

I said, "Yup, I'm missing both of mine, too!"

We also had internal fuel, so there wasn't any problem.
But fifteen minutes later, people were calling up and
asking, "Hey, did you guys lose something?" The story was
catching up to us real quick.

Shortly afterwards, Munns was given a new call sign, "Gus" (as in Gus Grissom), to pay tribute to his "right stuff" maneuver.

But beyond a doubt, the Silver Fox who scored the squadron's "first of all Gulf War firsts" was none other than Munn's sidekick, Bombardier-Navigator "Ploofer" Ploof, who, reputedly, sank the first *restaurant* of Desert Storm:

> There was a restaurant in Kuwait City right near the harbor. And there was a bunch of ships—one of them was a wooden ship. Only, it was actually a restaurant. They had pulled it in and beached it. But from the *air*, it looked like a ship.
>
> Apparently, *somebody* [everyone pointed at Ploofer] went in there and bombed the hell out of this restaurant.

"Must have served bad food," chuckled Munns.

A few days later, when a photo reconnaissance mission flew over the area, the restaurant was still burning—but all of the other ships around it were doing just fine.

According to Lt.(jg) Ron Ravello, a Silver Fox crew flew into Kuwait City right after the ceasefire and videotaped the restaurant for BDA. "They got a perfect view of this restaurant-ship," he said, "with a bomb hole right in the middle of it. It was a perfect shot, right in the center where the bridge [or the salad bar?] would be. So XO Munns claimed it as a kill for one of his bombing raids."

Then Munns cut in, "A kill's a kill!"

"But, by the way," said Ploofer, "for the record, we *really* didn't do it."

"We get *blamed* for a lot of things," added Munns, "but it's all just hearsay!"

Iraqis Couldn't Kill It

It took a while for some senior Air Force officers to accept the notion that one of *their* aircraft could have a nickname as grossly unattractive as "the Warthog." But that's exactly what the A-10 flyers themselves had called it forever.

Col. Kas Jasczczek, wing commander at Al Kharj, said he felt the name made perfect sense. "The F-15 Eagle looks like it could be an eagle," he explained, "and the F-16 Falcon looks like it could be a falcon. But the Warthog's just ugly. It flies low, grovels in the dirt, and does its thing."

Appropriate words, I thought, from a Falcon driver like the colonel. The surprising thing was that the Warthog pilots agreed. In fact, they viewed comments such as the colonel's as pure flattery, because they didn't just *accept* their aircraft's ugliness, they *gloried* in it. In a service bursting at the seams with sleekly sculptured, graciously appointed fast-movers, this was their badge of distinction.

And in a typically A-10 way of flaunting this badge, they showed me a series of cartoon caricatures of their plane. In them, all of the A-10's repulsive features were exaggerated to the point where the aircraft actually did resemble its namesake, the Warthog:

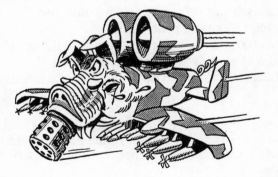

But in the Gulf, the A-10's badge of distinction was threatened with extinction, thanks to the advent of the stealthful F-117, the mysterious "Black Plane." Capt. Joe Davis, an Air Force PAO in Riyadh—who obviously did not appreciate the glory in being ugly— said he was sure the A-10 guys were glad to have the Stealths around, "since now the Warthog isn't the ugliest thing in the sky."

"Don't bet on it," I said, knowing by then something about Warthog philosophy.

Still, in a combat zone like the Gulf, beauty—or the lack of it—was not a real test of merit. Other characteristics meant a whole lot more. For the F-15s of the 335th, it was the uncanny precision of their laser bombing, and their video capability for recording it.

The Warthogs, too, could loft bombs with the best, but they were as short on video as on good looks. Then again, the A-10 never was designed to be a TV star. While it did have two camera systems on board that might have been used for collecting shots of its raids, it just wasn't practical.

To employ the Warthog's *gunsight* camera, for instance, a pilot had to keep his nose pointed at his target for a considerable length of time. "But we weren't in the movie producing business," said Maj. Sonny "Sun Dog" Rasar, of the 706th Cajuns, "and the bad guys were still shooting back at us!"

A second, and equally unwieldy system, would work only if a Warthog fired *two* missiles at the same target instead of one. Since its video targeting apparatus shut down automatically prior to missile impact, only a second missile fired in sequence would complete the whole picture of the first hit. This approach was also considered dangerous, and damn wasteful besides, so the pilots were forbidden to use it.

No, the true test in the war for the A-10 was neither in its looks or its video, but in its much vaunted survivability-under-fire. The Warthog was *expected* to take hits. Its low-level, tank-busting tactics almost guaranteed it. So the plane had been built with cable backups to its hydraulic controls and a bullet-proof titanium "bath-tub" in its cockpit for pilot protection.

Well, the A-10 passed its survival test with flying colors, to which Cajun Col. Jim Rose was only too happy to testify. His wing man, "Sun Dog" Rasar, recalled the day the colonel's Warthog was badly shot up:

I didn't actually see Jim get hit, but I noticed he was flying off lower than he should've been. I called for him a couple of times on one of the three radios, but, in his plane, that radio was broken.

Finally, I raised him on another one and asked, "What's going on?" He told me he'd had a dual hydraulic failure. He was flying with the backup cable system, but he thought he had the airplane under control. Jim was in a world of hurt, so I got in position to monitor what he was doing, and to cover him if some bad guy started shooting.

At that point, he was forty miles behind enemy lines,

heading north. His airplane was just barely controllable, and he didn't want to do anything too fancy, so I got him into a slow, climbing turn southbound and we headed out. I followed, flying big figure-eights behind him, trying not to be too noticeable in case the bad guys were looking.

The A-10 was damaged pretty bad, but after some work, that airplane flew again!

Needless to say, when you're that far north, you want to get back to friendly lines as fast as you can. But when Jim got up to 230 knots, the airplane vibrated so badly, he had to reduce his speed. We were able to get to the friendly lines after twenty-five minutes—but they were the *longest* twenty-five minutes that I can remember. That dad-gum A-10 certainly proved to be as slow as they say!

Jim did an excellent job of keeping the airplane under control and he was able to land it without any difficulty. But they had to tow it off!

Later on, as I was looking the airplane over, I found that the lower vertical stabilizer on the left side was all shot up. That's what had taken out the hydraulics. There were also a lot of holes in the upper rudder, the elevators, the left side of the fuselage, and in both wings. It was damaged pretty bad, but after some work, that airplane flew again!

Then the squadron CO, Col. "Tomcat" Coleman, told me he was concerned that the A-10 might be on its way out. It seemed the Air Force was favoring other aircraft over the Warthog:

But the Iraqis couldn't kill 'em, and I don't think the Air Force will be able to either!

Of course, the Air Force *might* have more success, because, unlike Iraqi bullets which you can survive, the Air Force controls the purse strings. And when they start drawing those strings tight, and say the Hog is gonna go away, then I suppose the Hog will go.

But there are an awful lot of hearts that are gonna go to the bone-yard with it, 'cause it's one hell of an air friend. We'd rather have flown it than *any* other airplane that flew in this conflict.

Capt. Rod "Shaft" Glass had a little more upbeat view of things. "We could probably get to be heroes, even if we are ugly and slow," he said. "Not everybody in the States hates that ugly, nasty kid Bart Simpson!"

Big Sky, Little Plane

Ned Rudd had a theory, three rules to live by during the war, which he'd developed in the first couple of days of Desert Storm.
The first rule was, "The sky is big."
The second rule was, "Bullets are small."
The third one was, "Saddam is an asshole!"
And they must've worked for him, because he lived to tell about it.

> Capt. Chris Hill
> 335th TFS Chiefs

That was one "Big Sky" theory. There was another version, a more widely circulated *official* version which suggested, in essence, that you could vector one helluva lot of little planes through the big Gulf sky, with only a minimal danger of mid-air collisions.

This particular version had many advocates at the top of the chain of command. They *had* to advocate it, if they were really going to implement the "Funnel"—the narrow air corridor they designated as the *only* way in and out of the north.

Comdr. Bud Bishop, of VA-145 Swordsmen, explained how it worked:

> The bombing was going on in Kuwait and Iraq around the clock. Probably every ten minutes there was someone going in or coming out. We would anchor off the coast, waiting for our target time, and we'd see a highway in the sky—a nonstop flow of aircraft.
> It was a funnel, basically, between the Saudi border and the Iranian border, and we needed to get somewhere inside it. We didn't want to run into our own defenses, and we didn't want to run into Iran. So there was this funnel that everybody used to go in and out.

When I was visiting out at Al Kharj Air Base, Capt. Chris Hill, of the 335th TFS Chiefs, asked me to draw a cartoon of the Funnel as he perceived it—a stack of pancakes:

> On the bottom you might have A-10s, then the F-111s, A-6s, F-16s, F-18s, Harriers, F-15s, F-14s, and F-15Es.

On top of all that you might have the B-52s, and above those, maybe E-2s and AWACs—all stacked up together like little pancakes.

Lots of thinking went into the plan for the Funnel. But, before it could go operational, flight tests were needed to simulate the reality of so many aircraft of such different types in so little space, to see if the thing would *actually* work. The results were often pretty scary, according to Gunny Anthony Santo of VMA-311 who monitored the tests:

> The pilots were going out to test the overall command and air control system. There were hundreds of airplanes. I can't imagine how many in all. But they had this combined services air strategy and they had to check out the system to make sure it could handle that many.
> We had a few of our pilots up there, and as they were flying north into the training area, they went into what we called "Midnight"—which meant no lights except for the dials in the cockpit.
> Control said things were getting really confused and overloaded, so they asked all the pilots to drop their gear and turn on their landing lights—then they could get an idea of just how many airplanes were around.
> When the order came to do this, the *whole sky* lit up. There were planes *everywhere*. This scared all the pilots, so flight control screamed, *"Turn your lights off! Turn your lights off! Everyone turn your lights off!"*
> They were a lot safer not knowing who else was up there!

Then came the night the Air War began. And with it, to add to an already hectic Funnel scenario, came the SCUD attacks. Lt. Ken Stefanek, of the Fighting 69th TFS, told me of a mission his squadron was on when the first SCUD appeared:

> The very first night of the war, nobody really knew what was going on. Our guys all flew into King Fahd to get gas, then took off again to drop their bombs up north. While they were in-bound, the first SCUD hit—it was four in the morning, local time. Suddenly they heard, "This is Dharan tower! We are evacuating! You are on your own!"

But SCUDs and military aircraft weren't all that filled the sky that night. Stefanek continued:

> A little later our guys were flying over the Gulf, when the Dharan tower returned and said, "So-and-so, so-and-so!"

There were some close calls, but the people who controlled the air did a fantastic job.

You are approaching a US Navy warship operating in international waters in a war zone."

And then they heard an excited Indian voice say, *"This is India Air Three-Two-Two! Don't worry! I am turning around!"*

But, once the war was underway, flying the Funnel became fairly routine—if you could call "being so scared, so often that it became second nature" routine. Lt. "Ploofer" Ploof of the Silver Foxes knew the feeling well, and so did the Hawkeye aviators who guided him through it:

> Our guys always flew with lights out. And a lot of times, when we came back from our strikes, our E-2 controllers would tell us that we didn't want to know how many airplanes were working in that particular area. They said we just didn't want to know, because there were a *lot!*

Ens. "McFly" McAlexander, who flew with the E-2s on combat surveillance and was privy to sordid details of the traffic congestion, praised the flyers who drove on relentlessly to their targets:

> From the first days of the war, we'd all been studying this "Kuwait" place and worrying about how we'd be able to strike in there. But you'd see these airplanes going up north, and they'd keep going up north. And they'd go *way* up north. Those guys had some big balls, because they didn't realize we had such air superiority!
>
> But we *owned* it. You'd look at the scope, and it would just be swarming with aircraft. And they were all ours. Kuwait was an endless racetrack.

Still, even the routine of the Funnel went to hell when, due to foul weather or an increased SAM threat, the flight ceiling dropped. As Capt. Chris Hill put it, "The big sky theory loses something when everybody's down at five hundred feet!"

Given the variety of flying objects in the Funnel day and night, good weather and bad, it was truly miraculous that not a *single* air collision occurred. But the war prompted other worries as well. Worries that compounded the routine grief of "trying to find those itty, bitty pieces of sky without airplanes in them."

For the pilots flying CAP, there was now the added fear that, in the "fog of war," they might accidentally shoot down one of their own aircraft. For Lt. Comdr. "Spanky" Gennette, this fear was very real:

> There was so much friendly air traffic going in and coming out, it seemed more dangerous just to be flying than to be waiting up there for Iraqi interceptors.
>
> We needed lots of communication and coordination to make sure that we wouldn't target a friendly coming back from a mission, which was a *big* concern for all of our fighters.

Only it wasn't just the friendly CAP fighters that posed a shoot-down threat to the bombers. Sometimes the danger was a whole lot closer at hand. Lt. Houstoun Waring, of the 335th TFS, was flying as wingman on one F-15E mission, when things got *too* close for comfort:

> The first night, we went in at low level. We were all in these formations where we followed each other, using our Forward Looking Infrared Radar (FLIR) to keep track. When the flight lead went up for his attack, AWACS started calling out, *"Bandits in the area!"*

My pitter, "Bear," started tracking where the MiG was. But AWACS was still talking about it being fifteen miles away, so I figured I had time to do my attack and worry about this bandit when he got there. We went down, dropped our bombs, came off on our recovery turn, and they were still calling bandits.

I decided to get down low *real* quick, because one of your best defenses is to get yourself lost in the dirt.

So we all went down low into the dirt, and started rootin' around in it. Flight lead was about forty-five degrees off my left side, so I knew where *he* was. But Bear had figured out that the bandit was off to our left side and behind us.

All of a sudden, this jet comes slamming in across our FLIR, reading like a fighter! I thought, *Holy cow! This MiG is down in the dirt with us. That's amazing! How'd he get down here?*

Bear was yelling, "Auto guns! Auto guns! Snag this guy!"

The sobering thing was, that it was the flight lead who had come slamming across the FLIR! But we didn't even get it figured out until afterwards. We'd seen him come shooting across, and I thought, *Man! If that's the MiG, he can keep running that way if he wants, because I'm not gonna chase him down!*

Watching the attack can (the fighter) as he got farther and farther away, I realized flight lead had rolled out from behind me. Lead had decided he'd heard enough about a bandit trying to run him down and did a threat-react!

That's the *fog* and *friction* of war. But none of us ever shot without making sure we knew who we were shooting at. So, thankfully, none of us had to face knowing what it was like to shoot each other.

The "Big Sky, Little Plane" theory worked out even better than expected. Sure, the pilots had had their doubts and fears, but they couldn't argue with success. Nor could they resist expressing their appreciation for the guys who made it all work—regardless of the branches involved. On one occasion, perhaps his one and *only*, the Silver Fox's "Ploofer" revealed his gratitude for the Air Force:

Somebody did a heck of a lot of good work. I'm sure that it was the Air Force, with their massive computers and airborne surveillance. I never read of any mid-air collisions in the newspapers. There *were* some close calls, but the people who controlled the air did a *fantastic* job!

Howdy, Howdy, Howdy!

Although our military has often been characterized by some taxpayers as a thoroughly wasteful bunch of spend-happy spongers, this was not the case during Desert Storm. Once hostilities broke out, the funding critics cooled their jets considerably. No one wanted to shortchange the troops who were risking it all in the distant sands.

How inspiring, then, when I ran across some aviators on the USS *Ranger* who showed a real sensitivity for the military budget. These guys had effectively implemented a cost-cutting method of their own design. Lt. Tony Aneratti of VA-145 explained:

> We had a call that we would make whenever we shot a HARM (High-speed Anti-Radiation Missile). We used HARMs for self-defense, and for pre-emptive shots to shut down or kill the enemy's surface-to-air missile radars, especially during the first few weeks of the war, when we were a dedicated, HARM-shooting part of the ingressing strikes.
>
> If we saw any of the enemy's SAM (Surface-to-Air-Missile) systems come up, our job was to fire HARMs at them. We were really needed when our guys went in at a higher altitude, because the SAM threat increased up there.
>
> On one particular evening, the ingressing aircraft had already hit their targets and were coming back down through Dixie Valley (the Funnel). We were trying to be really stealthy, so we used as little radio communication as possible. We didn't even make calls to our guys for our HARM missile shots, like we'd normally done since training. When we saw a SAM system come up, we just shot our missile.
>
> When the HARM comes off the airplane, it has a really bright glow. Well, one time our missile went right past the lead aircraft's canopy. They must have thought it was an *enemy* missile coming at them, because they acted pretty scared!
>
> After that, we made up a code word —"Howdy, howdy, howdy!"—meaning that we'd just fired one of our HARMs, so no one would think it was an enemy shooting.

*We made up a code word—"Howdy, howdy, howdy!"—
meaning that we'd just fired one of our HARMs.*

The code worked great, but it got so that every time we walked into a room and said, "Howdy," everyone ducked.

By the end of the war, the Iraqis knew what it meant, too. So if any of their missile radars came up, we'd just call out "Howdy, howdy, howdy!" over our radio, and the Iraqis would shut down all their systems—which was our main goal anyway. We didn't even have to bother shooting a HARM—which saved the taxpayers about $800,000!

But VA-145's cost-consciousness was an exception to the rule. Most troops were entirely too overwhelmed with following orders and staying alive to get themselves involved in the budgeting process. And, given their druthers, most pilots would've jumped at the chance to fire some ordnance and take out some Iraqis.

For instance, there was the Harrier guy, who, after experiencing all the fear and loathing of a brush with some serious AAA, could not resist the temptation to blow *something* away—regardless of the cost to either the Marines or the Kuwaitis. He recalled that mission for me under a guarantee of anonymity:

> We were understandably nervous, since we were going into Kuwait to bomb what was called the Trenchline Road. It was a heavy fortification, with lots of trenches and bracketed on either side by big AAA sites. Supposedly, a lot of vehicles were bogged down just south of there, and we were vectored in to hit them.
>
> We flew up there, but the flight lead couldn't find any vehicles. All he could see was the trench. Then, as we got ready to drop on the trench, the AAA started coming up, *really* thick. The ZSUs (antiaircraft guns) were fire-hosing bullets at us. Tracers shot up past my wings and over my canopy. If the plane could have flown sideways, I would have made myself as small as possible.
>
> We headed back down south along the coastline road, just trying to get clear of the AAA. But, suddenly, the lead said, "Okay, I've got a lot of vehicles on the road! Let's go after them!"
>
> "Okay," I answered.
>
> So I rolled in on the road. I didn't see any vehicles, but I saw an overpass. *Okay,* I thought, *those vehicles aren't going anywhere!*
>
> I dropped on the overpass. The bombs bracketed it, but didn't take it down. Thank god! Because we weren't really trying to destroy Kuwait, just the Iraqis who were *in* Kuwait.
>
> When I landed, I had to do a lot of tap dancing: "Skipper, I thought for sure I saw some SCUDs sticking out from under that thing. There was *something* under the overpass, and that's what I went for!"

This young marine genuinely regretted he'd made that attempt on the Kuwaiti overpass. Later, I'm sure he tried to improve his image—and his *aim.*

The Red Rope Ranger

Every war produces one illustrious bad guy, who, through a mixture of daring exploit and circumstance, rises in reknown above all other enemies in the field. Hence, he is forever linked with the history of that conflict—particularly, in the minds of those good guys who fought him.

In the skies over WWI France, it was the Red Baron. In the sands of WWII North Africa, it was Rommel. And, on the swamplands of Desert Storm's Bubiyan Island, it was "The Red Rope Ranger."

Comdr. Denby Starling, squadron CO for the VA-145 Swordsmen, remembered him well:

Bubiyan Island, the large island just east of Kuwait City, was one of the first places the Iraqis took during the war. Almost every day we flew in and out over there. And as we approached, we'd routinely see small-caliber AAA coming up. It looked like some guy waving around a long, luminous red rope.

There was a police station on Bubiyan. It was the only thing on the whole island that was marked on our maps. It just said, "Police Station." That's where this guy was thought to be.

And every night, when we flew over, we'd look down and coming up from this police station would be that red rope of AAA. I don't think it ever got high enough to hit anybody—but, in principle, it just kind of pissed us off!

So that became the dumping ground for all our unexpended ordnance. Till the last day of the war, if we had bombs we didn't get off, that guy down there—the Red Rope Ranger—became the target.

I don't know who the guy was, but he probably took more hits than all the other targets in Iraq and Kuwait combined. Saddam shoulda taken him back to Bagdad and pinned a medal on his chest, because if there were Iraqi guys running, he wasn't one of them.

The day the war ended, we flew over Bubiyan Island, looked down, and there was still this little red rope of AAA.

Later, while I visited with Maj. Seth "Growth" Wilson of the 706th

*In targeting the Red Rope Ranger, our pilots had
also targeted a vast Iraqi troop concentration.*

TFS Cajuns, the Red Rope Ranger came up. He referred me back to
gunners he'd seen in Vietnam who were just as ineffective—*so*
ineffective that nobody wanted them replaced:

> In southeast Asia, they had various places around the
> air bases that they used for training gunners. Guys that
> shot a lot, but not very good. We called them "3-level
> gunners."
> One of the things you *never* wanted to do was knock
> out a 3-level gunner, because, if you did, they might
> replace him with a *9-level* gunner, who could *hit* what *he*
> was shootin' at!

I suppose, if our flyers had considered that point, they might
have eased off on the Red Rope Ranger. But, as it turns out, the
bombing of the police station had major tactical significance. In

targeting it, our pilots had also unwittingly targeted a vast Iraqi troop concentration, as Lt. "Franz" Bijak, of the Silver Foxes, discovered:

We thought Bubiyan was a swamp. We didn't know there was anything there. Our rules of engagement (ROE) had a restriction saying that, if we didn't know exactly where the target was, we had to bring our bombs back. Nobody wanted to kill any civilians.

So, when we'd go in and wouldn't find our target, we'd think, *Oh, crap! We couldn't drop our bombs!* Then we'd head back and drop them on Bubiyan Island.

There was only this *one* little blip, a radar significant target, on Bubiyan Island. It was a police post on the island's eastern end. So, four or five times a night, we'd turn back south after being unable to drop our bombs, and we'd look at their radar screens and think, *Well, there's a blip over there. Let's bomb that!*

We just wanted to jettison our ordnance someplace, and Bubiyan Island seemed to be as good a place as any. We didn't think anybody was there. There was no INTEL saying they had people on Bubiyan.

But, as it turned out, there was actually a whole *brigade* there—the Red Rope Ranger and all his Bubiyan Boys! We had been bombing the shit out of this brigade, and didn't even know it!

Nine days into the war, our INTEL intercepted some communications from the brigade on Bubiyan Island. They said, "Hey, Saddam? We think you're a great guy, but we can't take this shit anymore! They're bombing the hell out of us!"

It was hilarious. After that, we *purposely* went in and did some stuff.

Our Little War

Though many of Desert Storm's attack crews had been trained for low-level bombing, and were initially engaged that way, the Air War wound up being fought at medium altitudes. After Day Two there was no good reason not to go in higher. Our flyers had done such an impressive job against Iraqi SAM sites, Saddam didn't have a missile left to shoot that he could control.

Besides, the low-level raids were dangerous, given the enemy's massive AAA capability. After losing one of its Intruders to a low-level attack, the USS *Ranger* changed its tactics and ordered the A-6 Swordsmen and Silver Foxes "off of the deck and into the ozone."

But this didn't set well with Lt. "Herman" Ruth. He was the RIO of a Tomcat fighter whose driver now decided to take his plane *under* the bombers:

> The A-6s finally got smart and decided they weren't gonna fly in at low altitude any more. So, Dave "Possum" Culley said that we would take the low block in our F-14s.
>
> F-14s usually run in the mid-20's, but since the A-6s were doing that, Possum decided that we would run in the 18's. I was pretty opposed to it, saying, "Hey, they're shooting at us up at 20,000 feet! We don't want to be *down there!*"
>
> His response was, "If we see some AAA, we'll climb."
>
> That night we gave everybody solid altitudes, so they could fly with their lights off and not run into each other. As we were flying around, the Iraqis started shootin' AAA— and it was goin' off *above* us.
>
> The very next thing I heard was Possum on the radio, saying, *"We're climbing!"*

In addition to the directive on medium-level bombing, other rules were put in place to increase the survival chances of the aircraft. But some guys always had to bend the rules. In another case of "anonymity before glory," an A-6 bombardier recalled a mission when one of the rules was bent to breaking:

> There was a rule in the air wing: NO SINGLE AIRCRAFT OVER THE BEACH. The major reason for this was that if you sent one plane over the beach, and the Iraqis along the coast saw it, they could concentrate their fire.
>
> Also, when we flew, we didn't talk to each other over the

In the E-2, they were all cheering as this one plane headed out to confront the Guard on its own.

radio, because the Iraqis could monitor us. They'd know when we were coming and light up the skies. But the inherent problem in radio silence was that if the other three planes in the flight went down with mechanical problems, the last guy left would never have known it.

Well, one time four of us went out on a strike over the Republican Guard areas. We were carrying some laser-guided bombs (LGBs), which you definitely wanted to use when you could get them!

We got about 200 miles away from the *Ranger*, and then it got really quiet on the radios. Abnormally quiet. Usually you hear *something*. Suddenly, the pilot and I realized that we were all alone. You can imagine the expressions on our faces. We were now about 75 miles inland, over hostile territory, and the rule said we were supposed to go back. We looked over at each other and said, *"Fuck that!"*

There were some E-2 guys up there, the air patrol, keeping track of the big picture in the sky. And there before them were all these massive strike packages—ten planes over here, six planes over there, twelve planes over here.

But here was this one plane—knife in its teeth, mother and country, breaking all the rules, damn the torpedoes and full speed ahead—saying, *"Fuck it! This is our little war!"* and heading out to confront the Guard on its own. And, in the back of the E-2, they were all cheering, "Look at those guys! They're a bunch of idiots!"

So there we were, just running in as fast as we could go. We dropped our bombs, got the hell out, and have been *real* quiet about the whole thing since!

Fleur Debris

The following is a firsthand account of the Gulf War's greatest naval victory, as told by VA-145's Lt. Richard "Kato" Noble and Lt. Rick "Stump" Cassara, the A-6 Intruder "boat aces" who won it:

"Kato" Noble, the pilot:
We were sent out initially to hit a Silkworm site. This was the surface-to-surface missile the Iraqis had. It was a real threat to our battle forces. We had a load of precision laser-guided weapons on our aircraft, so we were extremely successful against the Silkworm installation.

Then we were turned over to the local controller in the northern Persian Gulf for Surface Combat Air Patrol, or "boat hunting."

We said, "Here we are. Do you have anything for us?"

They said, "No, we don't, so you are cleared to freelance in the hostile waters off Iraq. See if you can find anything."

So we turned the aircraft in that direction and soon Cassara became highly ecstatic about what he was seeing on his radar scope.

"Stump" Cassara, the bombardier-navigator:
I saw what looked to me like a big blip. *Big.* It was like a chunk of Bubiyan Island had finally got knocked off and was sailing out.

We had been up there enough so that we were pretty much able to tell what was what. There were various blips that we recognized as wrecked boats and oil platforms. But this big blip was a large radar return where I hadn't seen anything before, and as we grew closer, it broke out into four distinct little blips, steaming in a four-ship, column formation.

Even before I got a look at them in the infrared, it was obvious to me that we'd found four Iraqi military ships, because nobody else steams around in that kind of formation. Nobody else is *stupid* enough.

The ships weren't coming in our direction, however. They were heading toward Iranian waters, as a part of the "flee or die program." And because there had been some rumors that the Iranians were escorting Iraqi ships into

109

Iranian territory, we were concerned that there might be an Iranian ship in the group, as well.

Noble:

We didn't want to bring Iran into the war. We didn't want that responsibility on *our* shoulders. If they'd only *shot* at us, that would have made our decision a lot easier. But they weren't helping us much.

The bottom line on the Iraqi Navy's
"flee or die" program.

Cassara:

It was night out, and they didn't have their running lights on, which was highly unusual. So we rolled out a flare to see what kind of combatants they were. But the conditions weren't too great. If it's too humid, you don't get very sharp definition.

Besides, the French, the Germans and the Italians built boats for all the countries in this part of the world. A boat of one type might be owned by any of them. So even when we looked through the infrared, there was some interpreting to be done.

So we made a couple of passes at low altitude, where we were very vulnerable. Once they heard our jet noise, they might start shooting at us. But they just kept truckin' right along.

Noble:

After numerous passes by us, they knew some jet was doing recon on them. I think they were just hoping that we would go away.

Cassara:

I was concentrating on the leader, because he looked like the biggest one. Then we identified him as a *definite* bad guy. It was a Kuwaiti boat that the Iraqis had taken over. Immediately, I called our controller and he said that it was up to us whether we shot or not.

We figured, "Heck, we're almost out of gas, but we still have a bunch of bombs—so let's start the show!" And we did.

Noble:

On the first run, we dropped one of our two remaining laser-guided bombs. As we pulled away, Cassara watched in his infrared display. The bomb guided to a direct impact in the center of the lead ship! We had no desire to kill people, but this was a war, and that was one of our targets. So we got pretty excited about it.

But they weren't quite as dumb as we thought they were. When we turned back in, one guy was headin' north, one guy was heading south, and the other guy had turned around. They'd scattered all over the place, except for the guy who was burning. He wasn't goin' anywhere.

Cassara:

The Blue Angels precision air-show flying team have a trick they call the *fleur-de-lis.* Well, the first guy was now doing more of a *"fleur-debris."*

The others still weren't shooting at us, though by that time it wouldn't have made any difference, because we were back at high altitude and just doing "dive deliveries."

I picked the next guy we wanted to hit and it was the same kind of run, and another bull's-eye.

We had a great airplane. All of the ordnance worked perfectly. And we couldn't have asked for a better set of circumstances.

Noble:

Except, now we were out of bombs, but not out of targets. There were still two of them left.

Then this wingman came up. He'd been targeting some Silkworm missile sites, when he'd developed mechanical problems with his delivery system. He had ordnance, but not a good platform to deliver it with. We had a good platform, but were all out of ordnance.

So, still having two tasty targets out there, we rendezvoused with the guy and set up a *buddy bomb.* We put him on our wing and made another run at the target. When we told him it was time, he hit his "pickle" button and dropped one of his LGBs. We used *our* laser weapons system to guide it to the target.

Unfortunately for the third boat, we got another bull's-eye.

But unfortunately for us—although our wingman had another bomb left and our system was still working—we were out of gas.

But, unfortunately for the last boat, a whole section of Canadian F-18s was headed his way, with a full load of gas and a full load of ordnance!

SCUDs! SCUDs! SCUDs!

*SCUD: an acronym for Soviet-Constructed,
Uselessly-Deployed missile.*

Capt. John Kostecki
8th Tanks

The sun set quickly in the Saudi desert. One minute it was there, the next it was gone. But when night came it could last forever, or so it seemed if you were living in SCUD alley.

The longest night of all for Air Force Sgt. Shirley Glaze was the first one she spent in country. It was indelibly etched on her memory by a series of SCUD attacks aimed at Dharan, where just that day she had begun work as a member of the Joint Information Bureau (JIB).

When a SCUD alert sounded, the standard operating procedure for the bureau's International Hotel office was to grab one's CB gear and rush down to the hotel basement shelter.

And so it went throughout that first night for Shirley, with alert after alert until the wee hours of the morning. Each time she heard sirens wail, she leaped from bed and, clutching her CB stuff, ran down four flights of stairs to the shelter.

Finally, during the last alert of the night, as Shirley stood there in the basement, dazed, disheveled and panting, a fellow JIB staffer turned to her and said, "For God sakes, Shirley, put on your gas mask—you look terrible at two in the morning!"

Whenever a SCUD alert sounded farther up north, in Al Jubail, the marine commander, General Boomer, grabbed his soap and towel, and headed for the showers—or so it was said. Supposedly, he did this because, with everybody else madly galloping for the nearest bunker or foxhole, he knew the showers were empty.

But Maj. Kent "Bradshaw" Nettnay, of the HML-767, began to read something else into the general's shower tactics. He figured that if anyone had the real word on anything of military importance, it was General Boomer. And if his generalship could be so blasé in the face of incoming SCUDs, it must mean that no one else had anything to worry about either.

This kind of thinking relaxed Major Nettnay considerably. After that, when an alert sounded in the night, he simply donned his mask and went back to sleep.

At first, the SCUD attacks freaked *everyone* out. But, eventually, most troops, like Nettnay, conquered their fear and pretty much ho-hummed the threat. I found this particularly true at Khobar Towers, an Army compound outside Dharan.

I was there interviewing soldiers on how they had personally dealt with the SCUDs. I turned to one fellow and asked: "What did you do in an alert, grab your mask and run to the shelter?"

"No sir," he answered, "I grabbed my camera and ran to the roof!"

But, even at Khobar, there were times when some troops couldn't share this soldier's calm. Just after arriving at the compound, one unit was greeted by a loud, persistent wailing that they took for an air raid siren.

Instantly, they grabbed their masks and raced for the shelter—only to discover the sound was a Muslim call to prayers, howling from the speakers of a neighborhood mosque. Once their heartbeats decelerated, these troops had a good laugh over the episode and went back to life as usual.

There were other individuals, however, who never quite relaxed enough to laugh it off. One bunch of soldiers I encountered at the "White Elephant" compound, south of Khobar, explained how, during SCUD alerts, they'd always tried to act so cool—when, *really*, deep down inside they were scared to death.

Acting cool was also important to a soldier I met from the Tiger Brigade. His outfit was possibly the toughest in the Army, but he told me about a time when even he had flipped out. It all happened one evening as Sgt. Steve Phillips and his buddies were kicked back and relaxing:

> We was over by our Bradley just messin' around. You know, workin' out, doin' exercises, and everybody was, like, mellowin'.
>
> All of a sudden, the radio come on, and the CO was going on about how we'd just been hit by a SCUD. He said a SCUD attack happened in Dharan. We really didn't know how close we were to Dharan, but from our position I could see a big city and I thought that city was Dharan. I'm like, "Oh shit!" Still, I had to play it cool, you know.
>
> But we had one guy, a sergeant, who didn't have a protective mask—it was broke. It wouldn't seal. He was running all over the place crying for a mask. And we had another guy, who from the beginning was like, "Fuck my kids!"—but when we got hit by a SCUD attack, suddenly he *loves* his kids!
>
> I'll tell you where it really shook me up. These M-2 Bradleys have this trim vane on the front. We had some water jugs, bottled water, just sittin' up there. And I'm

Each time Shirley heard sirens wail, she leaped from bed and, clutching her CB stuff, ran down four flights of stairs to the shelter.

digging through my bag, tryin' to find my protective mask, and I'm scared up to my eyeballs!

The driver on our Bradley was PFC Butler. Suddenly, Butler closed the trim vane, and it burst one of the water bottles. Liquid shit come down on me like rain, and I feel the wet drops on me. "Oh, I'm dying," I say. "They got me!"

Slowly I walk to the track, get in the back, and I sit in the turret. I'm just sittin' by the turret door and I don't feel good. You know, I'm going through all kinds of symptoms. I'm dying. Then the CO comes over the radio again, sayin' Specialist Austin and all these people have been killed—they had a "nerve effect."

I'm thinkin' all this is real, and I'm cryin', *"Ahh, they got Austin!"* I was really doin' some serious cryin' in that track. That really shook me up. It pissed me off when I found out it was just a *drill!*

A lot of troops could have identified with Phillips' panic. But for him it was just a one-shot deal. For others it seemed like a never-ending nightmare.

A Seabee out at Fleet Hospital 15 told me he was so conditioned to react in fear to the SCUD alarms, he was going to have to demand that the fire siren be removed from his hometown courthouse. Otherwise he'd panic every time it went off. And this was no small concern for him, since he was the local fire chief.

The extent of the knee-jerk reactions that a SCUD alert could trigger was never better illustrated than by a marine out at the Al Jubail Airport, who woke one night to the siren's wail. In an instant, this guy went from a dead sleep to a dead run, busting a gaping hole through the buttoned-up flap at one end of his tent. When I visited with this marine, he sheepishly showed me the long rows of stitching it took to patch up the canvas.

While the SCUDs certainly did generate their share of terror, they also produced a lot of interesting tales. Here, then, are a few more SCUD stories, told by the people who lived—and often laughed—to tell about it:

1st Lt. Victor "Schtick" Duniec, HMM-261:
The first thing they said before we came was, "There will be no practice alarms going off once you're in country." Sure enough, we get there and an alarm goes off. You know, it was our first time in country and we were always hearing about how many different ways Saddam could kill us and how the SCUDs could reach us there. So the alarm went off, and everyone panicked!

We had our chemical protective suits, called C-PODs, which came in hermetically sealed packages because they only last for a certain period of time. And they told us, "Do not break your gear out until we specifically tell you to." So the alarm went off and people were running around, not knowing what to do. "Well, do we break it out or don't we?"

Half the people decided not to take the chance and die, so they broke it out. So half the people were standing in chemical protective gear, and the other half weren't. It was a false alarm. "Done and clear. They're just testing the system. La da da dee da..."

WO1 Jerry Orsbern, 1st Bn., 101st Aviation Regiment:
The airport construction workers here were really worried about getting gassed. Me and my battle dude, Mr. Hobb, were out sitting in the Apache one day while some of them were marking off the concrete to put the tie downs in for our aircraft. They asked us, "Hey, where do you guys get those gas masks? Do they give those to you?"

Eventually, most troops conquered their fear and pretty much ho-hummed the threat.

Suddenly, some popping noise went off. Since we were in the aircraft, the timing was perfect. We "gassed up," put the masks on, and those guys looked at us like, *Oh, no! We're in trouble now!*

CW2 Greg "Turbo" Turberville, 1st Bn., 101st Aviation Reg.:
There was a running joke in Bravo Company about one guy, named Jake. Every time he went to the shitter, it seemed like we had a SCUD attack. So we had to say, "Jake, you can't go to the shitter anymore. We're tired of putting on our gas masks."

Cpl. R. N. "Frenchy" Gravel, HMM-261:
We started a pool. Everybody put in a dollar and picked a time when he thought we were gonna have an alert. It started to get so popular that we had a pool that was over $150. The guys got so involved it was unbelievable. They

picked 8 o'clock, 9 o'clock, 10 o'clock, 1 in the morning, 5 o'clock...and then they had so many people there was no more time, so then they had to pick a time like eleven hours, eleven minutes, and two or three seconds!

Lt. Col. Dick Cody, 1st Bn., 101st Aviation Regiment:
This was SCUD alley, but we'd just put our gas masks on and continue to work or whatever.

One night, we were sitting here watching *Wild Orchid*. We had the unrated version.

Well, there was a SCUD warning, so we all donned our masks and suits, sat down, and continued to watch the TV. A lot of guys were foggin' up their gas masks watchin' it, too!

Shirley Hines, American Red Cross, Riyadh:
I told George I wasn't going to work again till I got a bigger pair of boots. The ones I'd been wearing were too small. I called them my killer boots. The new boots I picked out were two sizes too large but they were comfortable.

The supply sergeant said, "You're not supposed to wear boots that large." I told him I wasn't trying to make a fashion statement. The boots were just for walking, not marching.

On the way back to the hotel, there was a SCUD alert. We decided we'd better get there as fast as we could. So there I was, hurrying along in those huge new boots.

"Come on, Shirley!" George hollered. "Move those feet!"

I hollered back, "My *feet* are running, but my *boots* aren't cooperating!"

SSgt. David Hebert, 595th Medical Company (Clearing):
We were over at King Khalid Military City when the bombing started. Three o'clock in the morning—it was right on schedule. Suddenly we were called out to the bunkers, and we had to put on our MOPP suits, sit down, and wait it out. The thing was, I had to go up and find out what the story was. So I went up into the orderly room and they told me, "It's okay. Have everybody go back into MOPP 2. The SCUD went to Israel."

So I got all the troops back in the tent and said, "It's alright, guys. The SCUD went to Israel." And all of a sudden—BABOOM! BABOOM!

I yelled, "Welcome to Israel!"

Cpl. Bruce "Biff" Godwin, 2 AAV 2 MARDIV:
We were on our way up here. It was in the middle of the night, we'd just switched off drivers. Me and the

This was SCUD alley, but we'd just put our gas masks on and continue to work.

warrant officer were in the back of the track, just barely startin' to doze off to sleep.

Then we heard a major from 6th Marines come over the net in a very low tone of voice: "At this time...all blue trackers...go into MOPP level 4." I sat up and the gunner sat up. The gunner asked, "Did he say go into MOPP level 4?" I said, "I think he wants a fuel report."

Then we heard the XO shouting over the net: "Did you say go into MOPP level 4?" There was no reply, and that told us one thing. The 6th's major was puttin' his MOPP gear on.

So we suited up. About three hours later, after we got the "all clear," we were checking out the vehicles, when the very same major came walking down the line.

He got up on Tom's track, and Tom said, "Sir, the next time you say anything about goin' into MOPP level 4, could you please put some *excitement* into your voice?!!"

SCUD Busters

You're gonna love us when you hit the Gulf!

A Patriot "Duck Hunter"
to Army Capt. David Mallard
while en route to the Gulf

Before the first Patriot success, life wasn't all that rosy for the 11th Brigade ADA (Air Defense Artillery), which owned the Patriot missiles deployed in Saudi. It wasn't that good for Raytheon, the company that built the missile, either, or for the technical advisors it had assigned to the 11th Brigade. One of Raytheon's tech guys, Bill Sailor, remembered well when the missile was still unproven:

> We were glad to test it and find out how well it worked, mostly just to get all the skeptics off our backs. This was one of the "unproven" war systems. Seemed like everytime someone talked about new "unproven" systems, a Patriot launcher would appear on the cover of Stars and Stripes. I was glad to see them finally replace it with good publicity.

Few of the troops themselves in the massive Gulf deployment knew much about the Patriot except for what they'd read. And much of that promoted the doubts of Sailor's "skeptics." As a result, it was often difficult for the Patriot crews in country to get the support they required, in supplies and equipment. But, as Sailor explained, that also changed:

> We were unknown and rarely got support in a lot of crucial areas. We had one unit up north that was hurting for generator repair parts. No one would give 'em any.
> Then they shot down a couple of SCUDs and traded one Patriot patch for an entire generator. The guy gave it to them, saying, "You bet! If this will keep you guys working, take it! Take anything you need!"

As the successes mounted, "Patriot" became a household word. Whether the troops were housed in desert foxholes, urban barracks, or suburban tent cities, they spoke of the missile often, with real familiarity.

Equally familiar to the troops were the Patriot's distinctive sounds, the loud—*BAM!*—of its launch, and the resounding—*BOOM!*—

of its detonated SCUD. Air Force Tech Sgt. Charles Walden, of the 706th TFS Cajuns, recalled once when he heard those sounds, and described the ensuing uproar:

> A couple of days before the ground war started, we had a real lax period. Everybody was out playing volleyball and throwing frisbees. I was out jogging, when I saw that I was just about to pass the women's tents. I sucked my ol' belly in so I'd run past the women and look good.
> Suddenly I heard the BAM! BAM! BOOM! of Patriot missiles as they shot down a SCUD right over the compound. I started running faster, thinking, "Oh man! I'm in my shorts!" I ran to the bunker. Everybody else in there had their masks on. They were all shouting at me, "Get your clothes on!"
> It scared the shit out of me, so I ran off. I ran right past the women and went into the tent—the wrong tent! I picked up somebody else's uniform and put it on. It was *crazy!*

In addition to the protection they provided, the Patriots also thrilled our troops with remarkable light shows. There was no mistaking the missiles as they streaked skyward, hellbent to intercept—well, *almost* no mistaking them, as Senior Airman Dickman discovered at King Fahd Airport:

> One night, I was staying up pretty late, after everyone else in my tent had gone to bed. I happened to step outside and see—flaming across the sky—what appeared to be a Patriot missile launching toward the north. I ran inside screaming to my bunkmates, "Patriot! Patriot! C'mon, get up and put your gas masks on!"
> Everybody was asking, "What are you talking about?"
> So I walked back outside, and one of the pilots standing there asked me, "Haven't you ever seen an F-16 on full afterburner take off before?"
> Then another one took off. And I felt about two inches tall. I went back inside and told them, "Never mind."

As the story of the Patriots' success continued to unfold, night by night, the Pat crews found new perks afforded to them, day by day. "You're with the Patriots?—Go to the head of the line," became a standard one-liner wherever the Patriots' colorful patch appeared, be it in the PXs (base stores) or the local shops, the showers or the latrines, the fuel dumps or the mess halls.

The quality of chow also improved. "One day, the mess sergeant announced it was scrambled eggs for everyone else," a Patriot crewman told me. "But for the Pats?—Eggs Benedict!"

Maj. Jimmy Adams, the 11th's public affairs' officer, remembered another perk offered to Patriot people:

> We were downtown the other night, and a guy looked at the patch and said, "Hey, what do you do?"
> We said, "We work with the Patriot brigade," and he gave us 50 percent off on all the stuff we were buying!

Still, in spite of their nightly successes and all the attention that it brought them, Patriot crewmen maintained a genuine, personal humility. Dave Perkins, another Raytheon tech rep, found this pretty remarkable. But he was also impressed by a dynamic new surge in Patriot unit pride:

> Eight months ago, this group of guys had normal military jobs back in the U.S., in a peacetime environment. Then suddenly they were actually defending the lives of almost 5000 people, and the whole world was watching as the Patriot did it.
> I watched the soldiers' esprit de corps. They knew the importance of their potential. After the first few engagements, and the soldier realized he had a proven weapons system, the intensity *really* picked up.
> The professionalism of the 11th Brigade soldiers was impressive. There were times when I sat in the launch control vans and watched as the soldier performed his task. You couldn't do anything but feel proud, watching that guy. No panic, just quick reaction and decision making. They had something that was brand new in the military, and they picked it up quick and made it work.
> When it proved itself, there was a change in personal pride and unit pride. Now they had a cornerstone on which they could stand tall and say, "I really have a *weapon*, and it's a *proven* weapon!"
> They were proud, but they weren't *arrogant*. The war made them humble. They knew they were doing a hell of a good job, but they kept it in perspective—"Yeah, we did good tonight, but we have to prepare for tomorrow night."
> They were proud, but they never let their successes do their job for them.

As the war continued, the reputation of the Patriot soared as high as the missile itself. On one occasion, Major Adams had to laugh as a soldier began comparing the Pats to another military legend:

> This guy asked me what I was doing in theater, and I told him I was working with the 11th ADA Brigade. He asked, "Is that the *Patriot* bunch?"

Since Patriots were launched in pairs,
each SCUD probably "hit" two of them.

I said, "Yeah."

"God!" he said. "The Patriots! That's the only hero we've got in the war. The Patriot's more famous than—than Audie Murphy!"

I said, "You're not even old enough to know who Audie Murphy is!"

"Well, I've seen his movies," he said.

Moms are always the first to point to their sons with pride. The mom of an 11th BDE command sergeant major, Fred White, was no different:

Back home, people were saying, "We're proud of you guys! We'd never heard of the Patriots before, and didn't know what they were, until you guys got over there with them."

Then my mom wrote me that every time she heard the

Patriots were engaging the SCUDs, she'd run to the TV and yell, "Get 'em, Freddy! Get 'em, Freddy! That's Freddy's guys!" She also wrote that grandma was a big fan of mine!

But 11th Brigade commander Col. Joseph Garrett worried that people were beginning to take Patriot successes a little too much for granted. "When the SCUD alerts go off," Garrett explained, "people just roll over in bed and say, 'Oh, I'm not going downstairs—the Patriot will get it!'"

I could appreciate Garrett's point. Earlier, when I visited with the 8th Tanks, Gunny Cornwell told a joke that reflected the absolute confidence the troops had in the Pats. "The word was going around," he said, "that the SCUDs were really effective—they hit *every* Patriot they were aimed at!"

Another marine added that since Patriots were launched in pairs, each SCUD probably hit two of them. Frequently, the Pat crews were asked why they launched two at a time. Raytheon's Dave Perkins recalled one such question, and explained how a Patriot soldier fielded it:

An Army guy came up to me, knowing I was with Raytheon. He started telling me a story that he'd also told a news broadcaster.

He'd been out once telling these reporters about the Patriot and how it worked. They didn't know anything about it.

He even told them that once, when the launchers knew that a particular SCUD was going to come down behind a particular building, they fired one Patriot to blow a hole in the building, so the other Patriot could fly through and hit the incoming missile!

I couldn't resist suggesting to Bill Sailor that it was a shame the Patriot wasn't CNN-capable because, with a little on-board footage, it would have been a shoo-in for the "Most Popular Weapons Video of the War" award.

But Sailor informed me that this idea was *already* in production. "Only our system is a little more primitive than most," he said. "We've got an in-line mechanic who rides on the nose cone with a pair of Snoopy glasses and a home video outfit!"

When You Wish upon a Star...

We were coming in the back gate, and some Patriot missiles went off. We saw them goin' on the same level and altitude that we were at, zookin' all around us, and impacting all over the place. We figured, "Well, shit! We're gonna bite the bullet on this one!"

Sgt. Mike O'Toole
348th Medical Detachment

As the terror of the SCUDs eased somewhat, and people began grabbing their cameras as well as their masks whenever an alert sounded, it became the fervent hope of many troops to see one of Saddam's missiles intercepted "live," in front of their eyes.

CW3 Randy Stewart and Cpl. Dave Tetrick of the Mickey Mouse Club were two of the hopeful. But little did these two soldiers know that they would come close to being *part* of the interception itself.

This was one of those incidents that later provided me with two versions of the same story. And it was in the synthesis of these two accounts that a clear picture emerged of how it all *really* happened.

First, we hear from Stewart, the pilot, with the more serious and explicit rendition:

On 23 January, my copilot, Will Gill, and I were on short final landing into Dharan, and I made my call to the tower. They came back and said the airfield condition was "red."

We looked at each other. We didn't know what "red" was. I called them back and said, "You need to explain what condition red is."

And they said, *"The airfield condition is red!"*

"Look," I told 'em. "We gotta talk a minute. You need to tell me what 'airfield condition red' is. Do I land or do I keep going?"

His only comment was, "That's *your* option!"

And about that time, the first Patriot hit a SCUD above the airfield, only *five hundred feet* outside our left door.

It lit up the inside of our cockpit. The whole world came alive. All I could think to do was just get the aircraft on the ground. I went for the deck to keep the other Patriots from possibly gettin' ahold of me, and then another SCUD was hit, directly on top of us. It broke up and landed over the end of 34 right runway.

The first Patriot hit a SCUD above the airfield,
only five-hundred feet outside our left door.

There was a lot of *"Gee whiz! Did you see that?"* and *"Let's get our asses on the ground!"* All we could do was park it on the ramp, and put our gas masks on. But I had to land *first*, because I was the one flying it.

It definitely got our attention. We were lucky we didn't have any debris falling through the rotor system. But when I look back and think about it now, if a Patriot hadn't hit that second SCUD, it probably would've got pretty close to us.

You're not supposed to get caught between a Patriot

missile and an incoming SCUD. There was just no way to avoid it, because they didn't talk to you and let you know what was going on.

Cpl. Dave Tetrick, riding in back of the Huey behind Stewart, found more humor in the close call, and a shot of irony as well:

I was the medic on board. We were coming back from a training flight. The entire time we were talking about how SCUD attacks had become such a routine thing, and how some of us had seen them and some hadn't. The guys who hadn't were all very excited about the prospect, so all night long Mr. Stewart was sayin', *"Boy, I hope we see one! Boy, I hope we see one!"*

He was hopin' to see one forty miles to the west, so he could just watch the fireworks. But you gotta be careful what you wish for.

As we were coming in, we started talkin' to the tower. They were tellin' us "Condition Red," but wouldn't explain what "Condition Red" was.

So Randy says, "Guys, look out for us, please. I think we may have some SCUDs comin' in. Keep your eyes open!"

The other crew chief, Gene Ebert, said, "Uh, Randy? We got Patriots!"

"Where?" Randy yelled. *"Where? Where?"*

"Out the left door!"

The inside of a helicopter is no more than about six or eight feet wide. Well, the white light was so bright, I couldn't see the other crew members as the Patriots were going off outside our door.

And Randy was saying, *"I didn't want to see one that bad! Not that bad! Not really that bad!"*

Later on, we watched it on CNN, and, if you knew just where to look in the starburst, you could see the little anti-collision light of a helicopter coming through the attack.

That's one of those stories we'll tell the wives *after* we get home.

Calling Home

Smart bombs and night vision goggles weren't the only high-tech innovations to help win the Gulf War.

Considering the importance of battlefield morale, a lot of credit for our victory should go to the phone company and the great strides they've made over the years in phone technology. For the first time, frontline soldiers could reach out and touch someone back home—not from their foxholes, maybe, but close.

Phone centers cropped up all over the Saudi desert. And, except during the ground war, units were constantly being trucked in from forward positions to make calls. Granted, the cost of a call from Saudi seemed high by domestic standards. But when you consider what it actually saved in loneliness for the troops, in worry for families and friends, and in legal fees for divorce lawyers, a call home was certainly affordable.

Often, getting to the phone center was the easy part. Then came the wait. In some areas, lines of troops waiting for calls stretched out for hundreds of feet. And even after a soldier had the receiver in hand, it might take five or ten minutes just to get a clear circuit.

Still, once the connection was made, it was worth all the hassle. That is, unless the call was abruptly cut short, as it was for one troop of the 348th Medical Detachment. After a dozen or more tries, each time punching in the desired number and having the phone jabber back, "Please try again," he finally got through to his wife—only to have a SCUD-alert sound.

"I've gotta go, honey!"

"What? You just called!"

"I know, but I've gotta go!"

"Wait one minute—you mean, you finally call me and then you don't want to talk?"

"I want to talk, but..."

"Okay, what's REALLY going on? Is there someone else, is that it? One of them woman soldiers? A nurse?"

"I'VE GOT TO GO!"

"Well, you listen to me..."

Click.

Speaking of phones and SCUDs, one young marine was talking to his mom, when suddenly she cut in.

"Oh, dear! There's a SCUD heading your way! I'm watching CNN and it's a SCUD, dear, going right for you!"

He finally got through to his wife—
only to have a SCUD alert sound.

Then the marine heard the Patriots fire—"BAM! BAM!"
And the SCUD explode—"BOOM!"

This was followed a short time later by the squawk of a nearby loudspeaker—"SCUD alert! SCUD alert!" It crackled on for ten minutes after the attack had ended.

I also heard many stories about the news updates our troops would receive over the phone from the folks back home. It seemed the people stateside knew more about what was happening in the Gulf than the guys who were fighting the war.

One marine flyer, with the HMM-261, had been given some classified information earlier in the day and was ordered not to repeat it, even to the people in his unit. So imagine his surprise when he called home that evening, only to have his dad tell him all about this classified matter—and in greater detail than the marine himself had gotten in the *official* briefing.

The Storm
THE GROUND WAR

*Yeah, it was exciting—if you
didn't mind the taste of your
asshole in your throat!*

Gy. Sgt. John D. Cornwell
8th Tanks 2 MARDIV

Gloom 'n' Doom

It was a beautiful sunset, two days before the Ground War kicked off, and a bunch of grunts from the 1 MARDIV were sitting around outside their hooch playing cards.

But some troops found it impossible to divert their minds from the impending war and simply have some fun. SSgt. L. B. Frye suddenly turned to the cardplayers and said, "I want you all to take a look at that sunset. Enjoy that sunset, gentlemen, because it's the last *free* one you'll get. The rest of them you're gonna have to earn."

A little dramatic perhaps, but chilling all the same. Certainly enough to cool off the cards.

The sergeant was usually a pretty quiet sort of guy, so when he did say something, it wasn't as if he were bullshitting. No, his words would zing out and stick to people. That's why his comment hit those who heard it so hard, particularly Cpl. Wesley Cooms. "I just hated to hear that kind of stuff," the corporal told me. "I didn't want to think about it."

Sometime later, the same guys were sitting in the back of a five-ton, again in the company of Staff Sergeant Frye. This time he said, "Gents, look around you. Look *hard*. Look at everybody *deep*. And think about it. Tomorrow, they might not be here, but you'll remember that look for the rest of your life."

Corporal Cooms had had it. *"Man, Staff Sergeant!"* he hollered. *"Don't be saying that shit!"*

The corporal told me he knew in his heart that nothing was going to happen to them, and, down inside, the *others* knew it, too. "But those guys were *scared*, man!" said Cooms. "A lot of them were reservists. Some of them had just got married, and they weren't getting much mail."

So the corporal roused them: "Hey, Devil Dogs. Stick with me, and I'll bring you home!"

With the Ground War imminent, troops throughout the theater were getting the same message that Staff Sergeant Frye had delivered to his grunts, though often it was delivered in fewer, less eloquent words.

Sergeant Chuck Grow, a combat illustrator with 1 MEF (Marine Expeditionary Force), remembered such an occasion:

> Our CO looked at us and said, "It's my job to tell you that some of you men are gonna die."

*The gloom 'n' doom picture he painted
had everybody really shook up.*

Silence. Nobody said a word.

So he repeated it again. And nobody said a word.

He kept repeating it until somebody said something. It was like he *wanted* it or something!

First Lt. Mark Eichelman, the XO of a Tiger Brigade tank company, received still another version of the bleak forecast:

Before we ever went into the battle, we had a marine major come down and speak to us. He painted a big gloom 'n' doom picture of how Kuwait was going to be nothing but one big, smoking minefield—how all these millions and millions of mines Saddam had purchased at wholesale prices from the Italians were gonna blow our tanks six feet into the air. He had everybody really shook up.

So when we went up there, the entire time it was like, "What if this happens? What if that happens?"

The Iraqi armor was always touted as being so good, and they had such good equipment, and they were so well trained. But the whole thing was just a cakewalk all the way across the board. We didn't hit a single mine.

Not even the helo guys escaped the fearful lectures. 1st Lt. "Schtick" Duniec of the HMM-261 explained about the impact of a few carefully chosen words on his "Super Dude" crew:

Our intelligence briefed us on all the weapons that the enemy had. That was their only job, to brief us on the threat. So they'd come in every morning and—brief us on the threat.

After a while, it got really depressing because every day you were hearing about a new and different way Saddam could kill you.

One of the threats they briefed us on—well, that's secret, I can't talk about it. Let's just say there was a *certain* threat that was posed, a *certain* chemical agent. "So? No problem," we said. "We all have our chemical-protective suits!"

"Yeah, *but*," one INTEL guy said, "your suit does not work against this agent!"

Our troops responded to the "threat briefs" in a variety of ways. Some simply complained about having to hear anything gloom and doom oriented, then tried to forget what they'd been told. Others, who bought into the briefings, were often driven to bizarre responses.

Such was the case with two soldiers from the 595th Medical Company (Clearing), who were pretty stressed out—or, as Lt. Butler would put it, "pretty stupid"—on Ground War Eve.

These young enlisted-types began burning cigarettes into their arms. When Sgt. Stuart "Woodsy" Morris asked them to explain what they were doing, they answered, "Well, you gotta be ready for any kind of pain!"

That's what they said, but Woodsy believed it had more to do with going home and telling war stories about their "shrapnel burns"—in the shape of four Marlboro Lights.

"Drivin' Through Hell at Four in the Afternoon..."

Picture this. You're a Marine Corps reservist in Louisville, Kentucky, working at your job, raising your kids, fixing up your home, and, probably, planning for your next vacation. Would you ever in your wildest imaginings expect to be plucked from all that and thrust half-a-world away, to become the tip of the spearhead for the biggest tank battle since WWII?

Well, that's exactly what happened to the men of Alpha Company's 3rd Platoon, 8th Tanks. The following story chronicles their role in that battle, from their Gulf War deployment to their triumphant arrival outside the gates of Kuwait City. It's been written from the firsthand accounts of the tankers themselves, using their own words—only, for the sake of clarity, I've compressed it all into a single narrative voice.

*　　*　　*　　*　　*　　*

The Tanks

"'You gotta have faith,' that's what they kept telling us. 'You gotta have faith.'

"Yet back at Lejeune, every goddamn lecture we got for two solid weeks was about how we didn't stand a snowball's chance in hell against all the things we were gonna run into over there—like mines and gas and on and on. We called 'em *you're all gonna die*' lectures. I guess the brass got us prepared for war that way, but it sure hurt our morale.

"Still, once we hit Saudi, we had some spirit-building activities that got morale back up again. For instance, we painted graffiti on the tanks—catchy little sayings, like *In God We Trust* or:

> *Ready to fight,*
> *Ready to kill,*
> *Ready to die,*
> *But never will!*

"Everybody joined in, tank commanders and crews alike. And we all chose our own words, so each and every one of us had something personal to carry into battle.

"Our platoon leader, Capt. John Kostecki, had *The Main Vein* painted on his tank's gun barrel, because—like he always said—'once it started shootin', it never stopped.' And on the side of that M-60, they wrote, *To Be The Man, You Gotta Beat The Man.* That was the captain's favorite expression. He got it from the wrestler, Rick Flair.

"Altogether, there were four tanks in 3rd Platoon. All old M-60s. Gunny John Cornwell's was called, 'Panzer Kommen.' 'Beruit Payback' belonged to Sgt. Joe Crutcher. And 'Sand Booger' was Sgt. Scott Murray's. None of them were lean, clean fighting machines. They had shit hanging off them everywhere. That's what *real* tanks look like.

"But those 'gypsy' M-60s had the old sights in them. And the old range finders, where you had to put ghost images together to get the range. Most of the time during the war we couldn't use them— because we couldn't see. It was either night-time, or the air was too damn polluted for visuals, so all we could do was estimate. Basically, we were *shootin' blind.*

"Our tanks did have 'reactive armor' put on 'em. That stuff was supposed to ignite an enemy round before it hit the tank. But the only real reactive armor was by the main gun. Everything else—on the sides and the front slope—was fake.

"That's right, there we were, a lead company of the 6th Regiment, and we had *fake* armor."

DAY ONE—The Breach

"In the middle of the night, on February 24, we were listening to a newscast. The announcer said, 'It looks like the Ground War is imminent!' We all giggled, because we knew that in two hours we were going to cross the border, and that's what was going to *start* the war.

"When the time came, we rolled into Kuwait. There was nothin' in front of us now but Iraqis. Gunny hollered over his radio, *'Hey, Saddam—Panzer Kommen!'* The fight was on.

"We started taking small-arms fire soon as we hit the first minefield. I saw it pinging off a nearby 'tuna boat' [armored personnel carrier]. Then Marine engineers in the lead tank shot a line charge into the mines to detonate 'em. As soon as the charge landed, there was a *huge* explosion.

"Sergeant Murray's tank had the mineroller, so it was the 'Sand Booger' that drove over the minefield first, right behind the engineers. When he got to the other side, four Iraqis suddenly popped out of a hole. Seems the line charge had landed right next to them. In my opinion, it was these guys who'd been doing the shooting.

"They surrendered, but Sergeant Murray had a tough time getting 'em back over the lane he'd just cleared through the mines. He couldn't really talk to them because of the language problem. And they weren't about to cross over without some convincing. So Murray used a little 'small-arms persuasion.'

"Captain Kostecki heard the machine-gun fire as he was checking around for mines, and instantly thought, *Oh, shit. He shot 'em.* But when he looked up, he saw that Murray was only shooting at the ground by their feet. *Well, all right,* the captain thought. And, grinning, he watched as the EPWs [Enemy Prisoners of War] went stampeding ahead into the breach.

"Apparently, the mineroller worked, because all the Iraqis made it through okay. Gunny always claimed that the thing was invented by Winston Churchill for the 'funnies' during WWII. It looked like a big rolling pin on the front of the tank. And it must have weighed tons, judging from the way it would set off the mines before our tanks could hit 'em.

"Whenever mines were suspected, the call would go out, *'Send up the mineroller!'* Then everybody would crowd in behind it. Poor ol' Sergeant Murray must have dreaded those words. Gunny said Murray probably had the tightest asshole of the bunch, because whenever he heard, *'Whoops, land mines!'*, he knew he was gonna go forward.

"On the first day of the war, we received the most resistance. We took artillery fire, mortar fire, RPG fire, small-arms and machine-gun fire—practically everything the Iraqis had, except for gas. We even ran into an antipersonnel minefield that scared the shit out of us. We thought it was a heavy machine gun cutting through the tanks—when, really, it was just us rolling over those little mines.

"It was tough going that day, all right, never knowin' whether to shoot or duck. At one point, Captain Kostecki hollered at Gunny to stick his head out of his cupola so he could see better. *'My head is out of the cupola!'* Gunny shouted back. But all you could see was the tip of one eyeball peering through his sight.

"As that shit kept falling around us, some of it bouncing off the tanks, I know *I* was scared, and I'll bet the other guys were, too. But it never occurred to any of us to stop or turn back. It's not as if we thought about it and rejected the idea—it just never occurred to us!

"During the battle, a gunner usually would spot the target before the tank commander did. And, if he saw something moving, he might not even bother to call out the combat fire commands. He'd just start shooting.

"The 'right' way to do it would've gone something like: 'Gunner, sabot, tank!'

"The first word, *gunner*, alerted the crew that a target was in sight. The second word explained the type of ammunition needed—a *sabot* round. And the last word described the target itself—a *tank*.

"But the most you could expect that day was:

'Can you see something out there?'
'Yeah, yeah—I see a blob!'
'Fuck it! Shoot!'

"Later that morning, Sgt. Joe Exton fired up the first Soviet-made T-72 tank ever destroyed by Western ground forces. And he did it with a 'heat round.' When we'd gone through the schooling for tanks, they told us a heat round wouldn't take out a T-72. But Exton proved 'em wrong. He smoked that thing in a heartbeat—blew the whole damn turret off!

"All day long we attacked with our tanks on line, spreading a sheet of fire out from the gun barrels. At one point, just after dark, we raced over a ridge and, on the reverse slope, we found an enormous enemy arty [artillery] complex, with bunkers, heavy trenching and all kinds of vehicles.

"That's when we started 'reconning by fire,' blowing up anything we saw and didn't like—tanks, trucks, arty pieces, boxes of ammo. Anything and everything. Before long, the whole mess was blazing away like a bunch of Roman candles.

"Then, suddenly, over the hills around us came a bunch of people. They were Iraqis surrendering. They poured in from every direction. And, soon, more Iraqis emptied out of the trenches with their hands raised, leaving their equipment behind.

"I overheard somebody reportin' it in on the radio. 'They're giving up, sir,' he said, 'but I don't see any white flags!'

"Captain Kieper came back, 'Sounds like bad planning to me. They've had *six months* to prepare.'

"Actually, many of 'em *were* carrying white flags, made out of anything white they could find—t-shirts, underwear, you name it. Some of 'em even had white sheets. I couldn't believe it! I hadn't the faintest idea of where *I'd* find a white sheet out there.

"Some of us jumped into the trenches, looking for weapons, souvenirs—whatever. We found all kinds of grenades, cases of 'em. We'd only been issued two fragmentation grenades apiece by the

*Captain Kostecki hollered at Gunny to stick his
head out of the cupola so he could see better.*

Marine Corps, so we picked up dozens of 'em there. Good thing, too.
Later they came in real handy for droppin' in bunkers as we rolled on by.

"We also found lots of AK-47s—brand new, still in their crates. Us
tankers liked that Soviet gun. It was excellent at close quarters. It
had a folding stock, so you could hold it up in one hand and fire it
like a big, long pistol. It held a bigger clip of ammo, too.

"We turned the EPWs over to the TOW [Tube-launched, Optically-
sighted, Wire-guided] missile guys who were with us, then headed
out north again. But, next thing we knew, the TOWs had caught up
to us again—only, they didn't have the prisoners along. Seems these
marines were afraid to be runnin' around out there without tanks to
hide behind, so they turned the EPWs loose.

"'If they surrendered once, they'll do it again,' one of the TOW guys
said. So we went chargin' on ahead, still on line, still reconning by fire.

"Since we only had one radio frequency for all of Alpha Company,
everybody used it to transmit. Therefore, if a guy in 1st Platoon—way

over on the company's left—said he saw something, we'd be listenin' in and know exactly what he was up against. Then we could cover his ass. That was the advantage of havin' one frequency.

"On the other hand, once we got in some shit, everybody wanted to talk on the radio at once, and tempers started flaring—

> 'I get to speak first, cuz I keyed up first!'
> *'Get off th' goddamn net!'*

"Actually, though, it only got that bad now and then, when some serious shit was flying around, or you had exploding tanks behind you and prisoners up your ass. That's when you'd scream something into the mike—then, you'd go, 'I didn't know my voice could get that *high!*' Mostly, it was surprising how calm everybody was in their transmissions. Real calm."

DAY TWO—The Ice Cube Tray

"We had three maps with us, but we were moving so far in such a short time, we had to paste 'em all together. We'd gone about 40 klicks [km] in a day and a half, just running and shooting.

"Later, Colonel Young, our battalion CO, told us that whenever he didn't know which way to go, he'd just follow the burning vehicles and the flashes from Alpha Company's guns.

"On the first day, it had been cloudy and rainy. The next day it kinda cleared up, till these clouds rolled in—big, slow, flat, black clouds.

"It was sorta like tornado weather, or like one of those line storms moving over Kansas. One minute it was clear, the next it was just black, and we couldn't see more than 300 meters in any direction. It was as if this huge inverted bowl had descended over us. And out past the bowl's edge was—*nothing!* It was like drivin' through Hell at four in the afternoon.

"Sometimes, we'd pass by the oil fires themselves—the cause of this journey into darkness. They were unbelievable, like roaring towers of flame comin' up on all sides of you. Captain Kostecki said the blazing wells made him feel like he was standing on a monstrous birthday cake in a big darkened room.

"Even Gunny, who was usually so good with words, couldn't think of how to adequately describe it—except to say that now he knew what 'nuclear winter' was like.

"So, that day we moved along more slowly, groping through the blackness till some weird shape would appear in the oily mist, then become a scraggy hill or a broken, twisted car. We never knew what was laying for us out there, but we kept driving—and all these eerie things would float on past us.

"At that point somebody could have called Alpha Company over the radio and said that a column of twenty-one T-72s were comin' down the road at us, and we wouldn't have known the difference. We couldn't see shit. We knew there were friendly units on both sides of us, but we couldn't even see *them!*

"Once, after rolling a while, we halted to wait for those friendlies, thinking maybe we were just too far out in front to see 'em. Suddenly, Gunny opened fire on a target ahead. His gunner had spotted a change in the darkness. It had gone from dark to darker, then back to dark again. They couldn't figure it out, but finally decided to shoot.

"When a heat round goes downrange and hits a dirt mound or a sandbagged bunker, there's an explosion, but that's it. If it hits hardened steel, however, thousands of pieces of golf ball size whitened slag fly off. Well, when Gunny fired, *slag flew!* So, he fired again and again. Turns out it was a T-72, just hiding out and waiting for us.

"Pretty soon we pulled up to what we called, 'ice cube tray.' That's what it looked like on the map—a double row of eight or ten little squares. From where we sat, it appeared to be some kind of compound, with buildings, trucks and bunkers. And surrounding it was a chain-link fence.

"Just then Gunny spotted a blob. It must have been a truck loaded with tank rounds because, when Gunny fired it up, it burst into a gigantic fireball. And beside the truck, in the light of the explosion, we could see four dug-in Iraqi tanks. That's when the term 'overkill' went into effect. The whole company opened up on those four suckers, hitting each of them at least five or six times!

"I saw Captain Kostecki climb out of his tank with his camera in hand, just as the turret blew off a T-72. The captain's always had a tendency to watch a while first, before snappin' a picture, so I doubt he got anything there. Too bad. It was a hell of a sight.

"Then, out of a bunker near the blazing armor, came thirteen Iraqi tankers, wanting to surrender. I don't really know if they'd been in there resting, or hiding out, because we didn't take time to ask any questions. We just passed 'em off to a squad of infantry grunts and got movin' again.

"We rolled right over the chain-link fence and started blasting away at all the vehicles in the compound. There weren't any more tanks, but there were plenty of trucks and jeeps to shoot at. And over the radio I could hear the guys talkin' about their kills.

"'What'd ya hit? What'd ya hit?' asked one guy.

"'I think I hit a Toyota!' said another.

"As we pushed on through, we tried to stay on line, but it was tough going because of the buildings. At one point we even had to form up in a column, bumper to bumper, just to get past. We were in together so tight, a guy could have hopped from one tank to another. And I remember thinking to myself, *This is not how you'd want the enemy to find you!*—because if they'd attacked us then, with our tank guns jammed in too close to bear, all we would've had to defend ourselves with was hand grenades and carbines—and Gunny's shotgun, *Pukin' Beulah.* On top of that, it was dark. So dark, you literally couldn't see your hand in front of your face.

"Suddenly, my worst fears seemed to be coming true—we sensed some movement up ahead. And, before long, with all the fireworks goin' off, we could make out people. Lots of people. When we'd pulled into the compound, it had looked abandoned, but now Iraqi soldiers came pourin' out from everywhere—the bunkers, the trenches, the buildings—only, thank God, they were giving themselves up!

"That compound must have housed a brigade-sized element, because among those EPWs were a bunch of guys dressed in little chemical outfits, just like our MOPP suits. They were older folks, too. And nine out of ten were married. At least they wore wedding rings.

"It was really surprising to see so many give up to us. We'd heard about other EPWs who would *never* surrender to tankers, because we were 'madmen' who shot everything in sight. Some were even calling us the 'angels of death.' Still, here they came—in droves.

"At first we had a lot of compassion for those guys. But then, when we had some of 'em spread out on the ground, and saw that they were wearing Rolex Citizens, all-gold watches—well, then we realized who we'd captured. So the compassion changed. We didn't hurt 'em, but we didn't care about 'em so much anymore. After all, they'd raped the place!

"Since a built-up area like the 'ice cube tray' was not a healthy place for tanks, especially with Marine infantry grunts moving up from behind, we drove north again till we reached the outskirts of the complex. That's where we figured to settle in for the night. But there still was lots of activity going on around us.

"As our grunts had come up, they'd got into a firefight with themselves. For three hours or more, they lobbed rounds back and forth—non-stop. Luckily, nobody was hurt, except for Captain Kostecki's loader, LCpl. Eli Jewell, who was nicked in the head.

"So much had happened that day, I found it really hard to get to sleep. But, finally, I drifted off with thoughts of my wife and kids, and happier times."

DAY THREE—The Chicken Farm

"Things got pretty lax on the third day. We didn't get rolling till about 1300. Then we met virtually no resistance, as we rolled on north blasting anything that crossed our sights. Fortunately for the Iraqis, most of 'em were buggin' out before we got in range. And, fortunately for us, the Iraqi tanks we encountered were always abandoned.

"I know I shouldn't say it, but it was damn good fun blasting away at those empty vehicles. Like kids in a shootin' gallery. I doubt we passed a single one that we didn't fire up—several times over.

"Still, once in a while, we'd hear some traffic over the radio about *semi-manned* armor in the area, tanks with just one guy in 'em. Seems the other guys would split, leaving the lowest ranking individual to stand off the 'madmen' Marines alone—sorta like the one-legged man at the ass kickin' contest.

"This was also the day that we ran out of map, somewhere about 11 klicks west of Kuwait City, near a place we called the 'Chicken Farm.' From just south of it we could see a berm, and behind it was this little bunker-lookin' thing with what appeared to be an Iraqi flag flying from it. We couldn't make that flag out too good, but it *was* the Iraqi colors—green, red, white and black. And off in the distance we could see a few tanks. It sure looked hostile, so we cut loose with a few rounds just to check it out.

"Well, wouldn't you know it? The flag wasn't Iraqi, but Kuwaiti. And it wasn't a bunker, but a chicken coop. It was sorta embarrassing, but pretty funny, too. One of the company officers hauled down the flag and took it with him—a souvenir of the most heavily out-gunned chicken coop in history.

"We reached the highway that evening, the Sixth Ring Beltway that ran southeast into Kuwait City. There, Alpha Company was split up for the first time, with 3rd Platoon headin' toward the Kuwaiti capital. Our orders were to stop all vehicles tryin' to escape—especially the looters.

"None of us will ever forget that night, the last one of the war. But I'm sure what Captain Kostecki remembers most about it isn't the five BMPs he shot as we turned east. No, I'll bet he best remembers the final 400 meters of that ride—and the *three* long hours it took to drive them!

"As usual, it was a pitch black night. We couldn't see shit. And, as the captain led us down that last stretch of highway—slowly creepin' along, inch by scary inch, those 400 meters seemin' more like 10,000—poison gas began to form inside his tank. But it wasn't Iraqi poison. It was his turret motor burning up, filling his tank with a toxic cloud of fumes till finally he was forced to pull off the road, where he and his crew jumped out. That was when the looters came.

There was this little bunker-lookin' thing with what appeared to be an Iraqi flag flying.

"You couldn't see them coming, you could only hear them. They were running up the highway straight at us, and movin' fast, hellbent for Bagdad with their spoils. They came with their lights off, but those racing Toyota engines gave 'em away. Well, our orders were to stop them. And stop them we did. Every one of 'em. It was our last action of Desert Storm, but Captain Kostecki had to sit it out.

"Afterwards, we took up defensive positions for the night."

The Parade

"The parade into Kuwait City began the next morning, with the Arab coalition forces driving down the Sixth Ring Motorway, right past the real estate we'd bought for them the night before. But our tanks just sat there, off to the side, still in combat positions.

"Later, Gunny Cornwell described the scene for some American civilians. 'We were supposed to be attrited,' he said. 'We were "dog meat" and not supposed to get past the first objective. But we made it. And there we were, with those diesel dinosaurs of ours, their big gun tubes and machine-gun ports all black from the firing, sitting asshole-deep in mud, and our worldly possessions hanging off them like gypsies. We were dirty, grungy, and tired.'

"And passing our *combat* tanks were all these coalition forces. Not a *speck* of fuckin' dirt on any of them. They'd probably never been off the road. And I just stood there lookin' at all that pretty shit.

"Only Alpha Company and a company of 2 MARDIV infantry got to see the coalition forces roll by. The Egyptians among 'em all drove Soviet-built stuff, like BMPs and T-72s. The Saudis drove M-60s like us. And, the Kuwaitis—all they had were APCs and jeeps.

"I thought back to our training, when we'd practiced for hours identifying the good guys' vehicles from the bad guys'. You had only five seconds to call one—'*Kill*' or '*No Kill.*'

"Well, the first coalition tank in the parade was a 'Kill.' And he was on *our* side. It was probably the last time any of us will see that again!

"A few days later we redeployed to a new staging area back down south. On our way there we passed through this little squatter village. At first, only a few kids came running out—but, before long, the entire town was there. We started throwing them our MREs and all our candy. I remember seeing this one little girl, who couldn't have been taller than knee-high and, beside her, this very old man. Neither of them could move too quickly, and all the other kids were keeping the stuff away from her. Still, she had her hands up to catch something.

"Then Gunny Cornwell spotted her. And though it'd probably been forever since he last played football, he lifted up an MRE and motioned to the old man, '*It's for her! It's for her!*' Then he winged that sucker back at them—Zing!—right into the old guy's hands.

"Then this other old guy came up to thank us for giving his

This Iraqi twenty-five dinar bill is typical of the souvenir money given to our troops by the Kuwaiti citizens they liberated. The inscription reads, "From all the Kuwaities in Kuwait. We thank U.S. army, British army, French, Saudi-Gulf army, Italian....We all fuck you Saddam with great pride! All the best, God bless you all!"

country back. He pulled out his wallet and said, 'Let me give you something!'

"Gunny Cornwell said, 'Oh, no! We don't want any money.'

"'But, you don't understand,' he said. *'I don't want this fucking Iraqi money.'*

"And he passed it out to us as souvenirs.

"Our company tank leader, Gunny Tony Rucker, was in a hummer filled with food and surrounded by a thousand raised hands. One kid hollered at him, *'What's your name?'*

"'*John Wayne!'* he shouted back.

"Other Kuwaitis danced around us with pictures of our president, chanting, *'We like Bush! We like Bush!'*

"'*So do we!'* yelled Alpha Company."

*   *   *   *   *   *

After the 8th Tanks had done such a remarkable job during those "three days of glory," no one could bad-mouth the reservists anymore. If anything, there was utter disbelief. When a reporter from the *New York Times* was interviewing 3rd Platoon on its role in the battle, he paused a moment, then turned to Gunny Cornwell and asked, "You're reserves?"

"That's right!"

"You're *reserves?*"

"For real!"

"YOU'RE RESERVES?"

"No shit!"

Colonel Young hadn't the slightest doubt of who they were or what they'd done. When he visited with the guys a short time later, the colonel, who looked a lot like Slim Pickens—a heavyset, jolly guy with a wad of chewing tobacco and a beautiful southern drawl—told them, "You're gonna hear assholes from here on out tell you what *they* did in the war, how wonderful *they* were, and how *they* won it.

"But you guys did it, and you *know* it. Yeah, sure you were lucky. But *you made your own luck!"*

Afterwards, Captain Kostecki added one more line of graffiti to the side of his tank: *USMCR and proud of it!*

The $4,000,000 Space Heater

*The Iraqis that stuck around got to see the Abrams tanks
up close and friendly, just the way we wanted them to.*

Maj. Gen. John Tilelli, Jr.
CG 1st Cavalry Division

The new M1-A1 Abrams tanks of the 2 MARDIV saw relatively
light action in the three-day Ground War, mostly because the 8th
Tanks' M-60s, which the M1s followed, left little in their wake for the
Abrams to shoot.

But it was a different story over on the 2 MARDIV's right. There
the Army's 2d Armored Division (Forward), known as the Tiger
Brigade, *led* the charge with their M1-A1s and, in the process, racked
up ground gains and tank kills every bit as impressive as those
scored by the Marine M-60s.

On another front, however, "The News Front," the achievements
of the two vehicles were considerably more lopsided. Everyone,
military and press alike, had his eyes fixed on the new Abrams.
Would it work as well as advertised? So, although the "diesel
dinosaurs" of the 8th Tanks proved themselves against the best in
the Iraqi inventory, it was the M1-A1s of the Tiger Brigade which
grabbed the lion's share of attention.

As a result, I wasn't too surprised to hear senior staff say that the
war was actually won ten years before, with the weapons procurement contracts that were put out—including, of course, the Abrams.

Tiger Brigade certainly did its part in building a case for such
thinking. Its Abrams rolled into Kuwait, firing on the move, and
knocking out scores of Iraqi bunkers and tanks, often at distances
exceeding 3000 meters.

"I don't think they saw us comin'," Sgt. Kevin Green, a tank
gunner from Alpha Company, 1st Battalion, told me. "Then, when we
hit the first tanks, the other crews jumped off and ran."

"We just went up the battlefield and killed everything in our
path," added 1st Battalion's S-3, Capt. Roy Bierwirth. "The Abrams
was just a wonderful piece of equipment."

***We'd just stick our MREs on the M1-A1's back deck,
and turn on the engine—an instant hot meal.***

In all, the Tiger Brigade destroyed 100 tanks. Alpha Company's First Sergeant, Robert Shanks, explained how his platoon alone took out 12 pieces of Iraqi armor. And five of those kills belonged to *him*. While naturally proud of his tank's combat total, Shanks' love for the M1-A1 went well beyond pride. The new tank had not just destroyed the enemy, it probably had also saved his skin, and that of his friends.

"After it was all over," he said, "everybody was going, *'Oh, you guys shot the most! You shot the most!'*

"I basically told 'em, 'We stayed *alive!*'—I wasn't thinkin' about numbers, but we shot some that might've shot somebody else."

On top of all that success, there wasn't a single combat breakdown. Clearly, quite a record for the Abrams' debut. And quite a testimony to those who promoted it.

Still, there were more advantages to the M1-A1 than its firepower and durability. But these advantages were not the kind that a weapons procurement officer would have foreseen. No, only a cold, wet, hungry troop in the field could have checked out the new tank for *all* its benefits.

"A lot of guys said that the most valuable piece of equipment issued was our 'four-million-dollar space heater,'" recalled Alpha Company tank commander SSgt. Jeffrey "Hey" Wire.

It was true. All around the Tiger Brigade, I found words of support for the M1's great heating capabilities. Sgt. Kevin Green called it his "four-million-dollar oven."

"We'd just stick our MREs on the back deck, turn on the engine, and we had an instant hot meal!"

It was also a "four-million-dollar dryer," according to Sergeant Wire. "Every time it rained and our stuff got all wet, we started one of our tanks up.

"Our infantry platoons didn't have the same kind of engine," said Wire, "and they'd all come trudging over. And we stood there, holding our sleeping bags and cots in front of the tanks, and they blow-dried everything for us."

But the heating possibilities weren't the only cause for the tank crews' enthusiastic endorsement of the Abrams. The *big* bonus with this tank was the sheer fun of its *SPEED!*

This tank could really haul! It was powered by a 1500 horsepower gas turbine, an aircraft engine, which would keep winding up and putting out more and more power.

Sergeant Wire's driver, Cpl. Peter Woods, told me a story that gave me a pretty good idea of what this power would do:

> Well, one time we had to clear the suburban area, and we were running our tanks right up and down the highways. I pulled onto one highway and there was an Arab in the car in front of me. He looked back and saw this big ol' tank, and he speeded away at about 30 m.p.h.
>
> So I kicked it up and speeded right up behind him.
>
> I'd say I was about five feet off his back end, when he looked back and his eyes got about as big as basketballs. He couldn't believe it! So he stepped on the gas again.
>
> And I opened it up a little more.
>
> The tank tops out at about 45-50 m.p.h. on the road, and I was doing about 45. He looked back the second time, saw me right on his ass, and he just pulled right over to the side and let me pass him. It was pretty humorous to think of what might've been going through his mind, seein' this sixty-ton tank passing him on the freeway.

However, in spite of all the M1-A1's wonderful attributes, the tank had one glaring deficiency—namely, no system for detecting the presence of nuclear-biological-chemical (NBC) threats. Actually, this represented more of an inconvenience than a clear and present danger, since the M1 could be buttoned up tight, creating a self-contained, toxic-free environment.

And, thanks again to Yankee ingenuity, some troops found the means to make up for the shortfall. Sergeant Wire gave me one example:

> In the tank, there's a space on the commander's control panel that says, "NBC alarm," but they don't have the alarm system in them. I guess it's for future development—they're gonna put one of these million-dollar NBC alarms in it.
>
> But, there are these little kangaroo rats that run all over the place. Well, one of the guys caught one and put it in a little co-ax box inside his tent. He was gonna use *it* for an NBC alarm.
>
> He was gonna take this little rat and keep it inside the tank, and if there was a threat of NBC and he didn't want to take his mask off, he'd tape the rat down on the top of the tank, and keep an eye on him.
>
> It struck me as funny, because we're looking at a $4,000,000 piece of equipment, and he was going to use this little mouse to worry about the NBC.

"I should be backin' up!"

"We were the scout platoon for 1-67 Armor," said Tiger Brigade SSgt. John Latchaw. "Our mission was to detect the enemy and inform the CO what he had up in front of him, and on his flanks."

Like most Americans, I'd heard a lot about the Bradley fighting vehicle and, at last, there I was talking with the guys who manned them in the war. It was a hot, windy, dusty day in Saudi, as I visited with those Bradley guys, all huddled together on Army cots in the shade of one of their machines.

"Our Bradleys were strictly nothing but scouts," Latchaw continued. "We were always the first ones to see the enemy, before the tanks and infantry. Then we'd call up the tanks."

At least that was standard operating procedure, the way they'd been trained to do it. But, as I listened, I learned that SOP was O-U-T once the war began.

"We fired them up ourselves," said Latchaw's driver, PFC Frank Ford. "I was real surprised! I was down in the driver's hatch, listening to Motley Crue's *Knock 'Em Dead, Kid*, on my Walkman. And I heard them calling us up, and thought to myself, *At least we're not gonna shoot at anything.*

"Next thing I know, the lieutenant goes, 'Fire them up! Fire them up!' So they raised the launcher and blew them away."

At this point I realized that once again I'd stumbled across people with a helluva tale to tell. Latchaw kept the story going:

> It happened the day after we breached the minefield. We were on a screen-line trying to find the enemy for the tanks, as they were maneuvering to get into formation behind us. The scout platoon detected four T-55s, an armored personnel carrier, and seventeen dismounted people.
>
> We all heard on the radio when the lieutenant got the word for us to engage the targets. And for us scouts, getting that order surprised everybody in the whole platoon. Our mission wasn't to engage targets. Our mission was to spot them and then try to make them engage us. That way, we could find out exactly what was in front of us.
>
> But with the distance that we had, and the TOW missile having a range of 3700 meters, we were the best way of engaging them.

As a result, Latchaw's platoon became the first out of his battalion to fight the enemy. But really it wasn't as simple as Latchaw made it sound. When they fired their first TOW, at a range of about 2300 meters, it missed. Apparently, the gunner overreacted a bit, making too big a "bolt adjustment."

When you launched a TOW, it was crucial where the gunner maintained the crosshairs. And if he rotated the turret on the Bradley too quickly—too big of a bolt adjustment—the missile couldn't react fast enough and would miss its target. The gunner was understandably a little nervous in his first combat firing and jerked things around a bit too hard. But, after shaking off the "buck fever," he nailed three kills for the next three TOWs.

Latchaw finished his account of the engagement:

> We could see the T-55s beautifully through the sights. As soon as we fired the first missile, they knew who was firing at them and decided to get out of the tank. But the tank was still moving, because the driver was still in it.
>
> It depends on where you hit a tank whether or not it takes the turret off. If you hit it right between the hull and the turret, it'll pop the turret off. But if you just hit the hull part or the turret itself, the penetration just blows it up and it sparks all over the place.
>
> The TOW missile is so slow that it took 13 seconds to go that distance. The platoon leader wanted to know if I was hitting them, because I was the only one that could see the tanks. And I said, "Well, the missile's still firing."
>
> Then I looked back through the sights, thinking maybe I *had* missed my target. Suddenly the missile hit. Everybody saw the sparks goin' off that time! And it was basically the same thing for the other two missiles.

As with the Apache helicopter and the M1-A1 tank, everyone had been waiting to see how well the Bradley would perform in battle. Up to this point, it seemed the final result would be similar to the others. Then, incredibly, the heroic saga turned into something of a horror story as, one by one, the Bradley's problems began to emerge.

"Right before we rolled out to battle, our commo went out," said PFC Shawn Moseby, who rode in a different Bradley from Latchaw and Ford. "Although we could still communicate with each other inside the Bradley, we couldn't talk to any other vehicle, our platoon leader, or our sections sergeant!

"We had to go on hand and arm signals from Sergeant Latchaw to move up, move back, or stop. So when the shooting started, we were on our own. Battalion was yelling at us and telling us to stop firin', but we couldn't hear them, so we kept it up!"

Chalk up one glitch, I thought. Private First Class Ford took it from there:

> The first day wasn't really scary, because they weren't even expecting us. But the *second* day was!
>
> We were out near these big oil tanks, and Sergeant Latchaw told me to drive over there so we could shoot at them. We started shootin', and the next thing we knew there were tanks and personnel carriers all over the place, and people running around.
>
> So we started firing the 25mm—*POP! POP! POP! POP!*—and then it misfired. Sergeant Latchaw and the gunner started messin' with it, trying to get it to fire, and arguing about why it wouldn't.
>
> While they were arguing, I saw these muzzle flashes from the tanks shooting back at us. I was sitting there, going, "I should be backing up now!"
>
> So the gunner switched to the co-ax machine gun and started firing again. And then *that* malfunctioned! And they were sitting there, goin', "Oh, fuck! Nothing's working!"
>
> And I was sitting there, goin', "I should be backing up!"
>
> So Latchaw yelled, *"Raise the launcher! Raise the launcher!"* And they fired a couple of missiles at one tank. But it kept rolling. They didn't know if they'd killed it or not, so they hit it again. It *still* kept rolling!

"Believe it or not," said Latchaw, "that was a T-55, so we must not have been hittin' it in the right spot. Finally, though, after it rolled about three or four hundred yards, it caught on fire."

Then Spec. Larry "Mac" McCarter, an infantry trooper assigned to the scouts, and one of the guys who loaded the T-55–killing TOWs, gave his view of the incident:

> Nick and I were in the back, looking through the periscope, when we started firing the TOWs. And every time the TOW fired, we saw the flash of the blast as it hit, and everyone in the track started cheering and yelling. Then all our weapons started going down. But as I looked outside, I still saw muzzle flashes.
>
> "Hold on," I said to Nick. *"We're* not firing. And there's no tank *beside* us that's firing. Somebody fired at us!"
>
> We started getting all worried, and every time we looked through the periscope there was a round goin' off by our track.

All I knew was that my faith in those fighting vehicles was waning

154

YES, SIR, WE'LL SCOUT AHEAD IN OUR BRADLEY — JUST AS SOON AS WE LOCATE ALL THE PIECES!

The heroic saga turned into something of a horror story as the Bradley's problems began to emerge.

by the minute. And that's when Sgt. Henry Lee Howard gave it a shot—sort of a *coup de grâce:*

> On our last attack, we were taking a town to the west of Kuwait City. As we moved up to our final objective, my turret gun went down. And our Bradley was the one that didn't have communications with anyone else—the one Moseby told you about.
>
> When Sergeant Latchaw's gun went down earlier, he had asked the commander if he could move back behind the tanks. The colonel told him that as long as he had his co-ax gun and he could talk, he had to stay up front. So when our gun went down, I didn't bother to ask if we could back up and just tried to fix it.
>
> The driver was pretty much on his own, trying to keep up with the whole platoon in the middle of the battle, as the gunner and I got down inside the turret to work on the gun.

We pulled the whole gun apart, dropping parts all over the floor, but we couldn't get it fixed. So we gave up on it, and I stuck my head up to look around.

We were in the middle of a junkyard. And sticking their heads up out of their foxholes were a whole lot of Iraqi soldiers! I thought we were goners.

Sadly, I tucked my head back into the turret. My gunner looked over at me, and when he saw how frustrated I was, his eyes almost popped out of his head.

There was a momentary pause, and we both started back working on the gun. Benton, one of our loaders, was sitting in the back, and he asked us if we knew the Lord's prayer.

I knew it, so I started saying it. Everybody else in the track followed suit, and we said the whole Lord's prayer together.

Soon we fixed the gun and started back to firing.

Amen. But then Specialist McCarter spoke up again and, in spite of all I'd heard, gave me a glimmer of renewed hope in the Bradley. According to McCarter, the fighting vehicles that these guys were driving weren't the *new* Bradleys, but some old ones. Maybe even early prototypes. Could it be that all of those problems were simply a matter of resupply?

Everybody else got new Bradleys. We were the only ones stuck with the old Bradleys, and we were in ancientville compared to that brand-new stuff. The only thing that the new Bradleys had that we didn't were transmission problems. But most of the time, when we went out on a mission, half of ours came back with broken down engines. One of them had to be fixed three or four times. Every time it went out, the same thing happened to it. And they tried to blame it on us, for not doing the proper maintenance with the parts they gave us!

Still, McCarter did find a silver lining in his unit's gloomy experience with the Bradleys.

"If we'd had Humvees," he said, referring to the vehicle of choice for most scouts, "we probably wouldn't have seen as much action as we did—and now we're like the heroes of the battalion!"

I said my good-byes to these troops, grateful again that I had shared some time with truly brave people. Just in passing, I turned to Moseby and asked, "Which is your Bradley, son?"

"Mine's the one in the back," he answered, "the one that's *broke.*"

I left those guys and headed over to Khobar Towers to interview some infantry troops, thinking that what I'd heard was probably only a fluke—just some bad luck for that particular bunch of scouts. But then, over at Khobar, I was offered one more anecdote about a fighting vehicle in trouble. Sgt. "Oakie" Rigney did the recounting:

> The first night inside Kuwait we threw a track, which is a very serious incident. Especially considering it was night time, and you're not sure where the enemy's at, or if they're gonna hit you or not.
>
> When you throw a track, you have to break the track and put it back on to the vehicle. Well, we had to take the side plates off with the power tools—which made a lot of noise. So all night long, for about ten hours, we were working on this vehicle—*CLANK! CLINK! CLANK!*—and all these loud noises.
>
> We were worried about the enemy, but at the same time we wanted to hurry up and get our vehicle ready to move, so, if the enemy did come, at least we could fight back.
>
> About seven o'clock in the morning, my platoon did an assault on some bunker positions about 500 meters in front of us, and we watched the battle like spectators would watch a football game—from the sidelines.
>
> And 300 meters to the left, behind our perimeter, we saw what seemed like thousands—it was probably more like hundreds—of enemy personnel swarming out of their holes. They just started marching in formation to surrender to another unit. And that's when we realized—if these guys had wanted to, they could've walked right over and whacked us! We could've been their first victims. There's no doubt about that!

Back in my Army days I helped repair a few tracks myself, on some stranded M-60s—just like those the 8th Tanks deployed. They say it comes with the territory when you're armor. So I couldn't help laughing when, later that night at Khobar, I heard the comment of one more Bradley guy—a master gunner, no less.

As he escorted me out of the Tiger Brigade area, he said with a great deal of sincerity and conviction, *"It's a great piece of equipment."*

Confusion Control

If you think the Bradleys had their share of problems rolling across the Kuwaiti desert, wait'll you hear what happened to a bunch of marines in the air above them.

I'm referring to a mission flown into Kuwait involving fifty-six helicopters, many of them carrying TOW missiles to form a "blocking force." When the waves of coalition armor penetrated the Iraqi barriers, these TOWs would protect their flanks. As with most missions, this one was based on a good plan. Only the plan changed.

The Wait

The worst part of the mission was waiting for it to start. As the crews sat in their helos ready to launch, a thousand worries raced through their minds. For many, it was a difficult scene to describe, but 1st Lt. "Schtick" Duniec of HMM-261 gave it a try:

> I almost had a "high" feeling, like I was inebriated. I was just talkin' to a kid from Montana about similar places we'd been and things we'd done, like hunting and stuff. But always in the back of my mind was the fact that, at any minute, we could launch—and within thirty minutes after that, I could be dead.

There were plenty of reasons to fear what lay out there. Aside from the massive AAA threat, numerous powerlines had to be crossed, many as high as 200 feet, and the plan called for a go-in-low approach. Then there was the unsettling prospect of flying in formation with such a huge air armada—fifty-six helicopters in close proximity, possibly with some itchy-trigger-fingers on board. Also, it was a multinational force, with Syrians involved, and no one was sure if they were *really* friendly. Just a whole lot of variables to consider, as the crews sat and waited.

Some, like Schtick, tried not to think about it. "Like the psychologists say, when you're a pilot or a crew member it's as if you're crawling back into your mother's womb—everything's real comfortable once you sit down. You go through your procedures and your checklists, and it's like any other flight."

Still, few could completely ignore the fact that they would be flying into Kuwait, against the most sophisticated air defenses that the United States had ever faced. More sophisticated even than in Vietnam, for the Iraqis had all the latest technology in missiles and antiaircraft guns. Even Schtick had to weigh the realities:

> I looked in my holster. I had a .45 caliber pistol, which was designed in 1897.
> Loaded in the back of my helicopter was a Willy's jeep, which was designed in World War II.
> And my helicopter itself was designed in the fifties.
> I said to myself, "I'm goin' in against the most sophisticated defenses in the world and the youngest thing on this mission is *me!*"

The Word

The mission was the "on-call" variety, meaning that everyone had been up and ready by 7:30 that morning, just waiting for the word. Schtick vividly remembered what happened after that:

> We were standing around, chemical gear on up to our necks. And they said, "When you see the white star cluster go up, run to your helicopter, put your gas mask and your helmet on, get the airplanes turning, and get ready to launch in 15 minutes."
> So we sat around all day, waiting. Everybody was kind of nervous, thinking about the S-2 brief on how many ways Saddam could kill us. There were a few nervous jokes here and there.
> Then, finally, we saw the white star cluster go up, at 3:30 in the afternoon. Our hearts stopped.
> We ran to the aircraft, started getting suited up. But we didn't start up our aircraft. We were gonna get a signal first—the next white star cluster.
> So here it was, 3:30 in the afternoon. We had our chemical gear and gas masks on. I mean, the suits are good by design, compared to anyone else's in the world, but they're still hot. And sitting in the helicopter cockpit, with all the glass around us, and nowhere for the air to escape, we had the old greenhouse effect!
> So we sat in the blazing sun, with our chemical gear

on, waiting nervously for the mission to start. We ended up sitting there for about an hour and forty-five minutes before the word came down.

And even then, it didn't happen. The word passed that everybody was to get out of the aircraft so we could have a hasty brief—the plan had been changed.

We hopped out of the aircraft. I took my gas mask off, and there was just a big pool of water around my neck. There's a seal that goes around your neck. I tried to take it off, and it got stuck on my head somehow. As I pulled the gas mask off, I brought the water up to my face. So then I was drowning in my own sweat, and I was still stuck.

I finally got my mask off, and we went to our brief. They said, "The plan has been changed. We're flying this mission at night, and it's not an NBC environment." Our attacking forces had got so far up and, throughout that time, they hadn't encountered one chemical weapon.

So we were going to fly our mission at night, with night vision goggles [NVGs] on. We manned up the aircraft, launched them, and got out of there, heading towards Kuwait.

The Flight In

At last they were airborne and, once launched, their fears disappeared. At least those that you'd notice. The crews were altogether too busy now to worry, concentrating on the job at hand.

"When I saw what it was like up there," said Schtick with a grin, "it didn't even seem like a war. I guess I'd envisioned war movies of flying in with tracers and AAA, but it was like just another flight."

Except that the whole world below him seemed to be on fire:

The only thing I can compare it to is looking into hell. *Everything* was on fire. The whole horizon was aflame.

It was so bright that my goggles—which magnify the light 20,000 times—shut down. They have an automatic brightness control, and compensate for light changes. Plus, there was so much light pollution that I was losing sight of the other helicopters. I put my goggles up, and was flying in the middle of the night and could still see all the other helicopters in formation. It was like flying into a sunrise.

People had been predicting for months that the Gulf War would give birth to the biggest tank fight in history, with unheard of numbers of everything from landmines to missiles, artillery to armor—the Super Bowl of tank battles, they'd called it. But from up above it, Schtick had a very different perception:

> I was expecting to see tanks dueling left and right, and TOW missiles being launched. But as we were flying over Kuwait, I looked down and saw *busses* driving north.
> I thought, "What the heck is going on here?" I flipped out. I thought it must be the Partridge family down there or something! But the EPWs were coming en masse, so they'd had to drive busses up there to drive them all back.
> We went further on, and then we started to see the tank battles and stuff. A tank got hit right below me, a huge flash. It was like lightning, it was so fast. It was pretty scary, 'cause it hit with such finality.

Up to this point, all was going as planned. But that's exactly when Murphy's Law is most likely to come into play—and such was the case here.

The Abort

As the helos forged on, they got the *new* word—the landing zone (LZ) where the helicopters had planned to put down was still under artillery fire. Suddenly, the mission was being aborted. Fifty-six helicopters in formation heading into Kuwait, and now they had to turn around. It was a scene Schtick will never forget:

> *That's* when it got exciting!
> If jets are flying in formation and they hit each other, tapping wings or something, they come back and land, scrape the paint off the wing, and laugh about it at the Officers Club. But if *helicopters* have a mid-air collision or tap each other in formation, it's very catastrophic. If the rotors hit each other, the helicopters just fall apart. It's not very graceful.
> It must be really tough for the crew chiefs because, while they see everything, they don't have controls in their hands. Plus the crew up front are officers, while the ones in the back are enlisted men and bound by law to be respectful: "Sir! Sir! Please, sir! You're coming in a little too close, sir!"
> You know what they really wanted to say, but didn't!

The helos began to turn south. It wasn't pretty. In fact it was more like a melee, with some birds going underneath others, some going above, some circling around to the left, others to the right.

Lt. Col. Rick "Pappy" Husty, XO of the HMA-775 Coyotes, drew me an analogy for the folks back home. "If you were in a parking lot filled with 56 big cars—and somebody hollered, *'Okay, everybody make a right-hand turn! And maintain formation!'*—you'd get the exact same result. People would be all over the place, crossing behind, coming from the opposite direction.

"And then just exaggerate that," said Husty, "by having it done in the pitch black night—*with the lights out!*"

But all 56 survived the turn, and 51 of the 56 helos headed for Lonesome Dove.

The LZ

At Lonesome Dove, a forward base for helicopters, there were precisely enough parking spaces for its routinely deployed Hueys and Cobras. That was it, except for what parking might be available on the small, makeshift landing strip alongside the fuel pits.

Even for the resident flyers in normal times it had been an ongoing struggle to land at the Lonesome Dove LZ, according to Capt. Marc "Ace" Richardson, another Coyote.

"Once you took off, you were lucky if you got to land in the *dirt* coming back," he said. "Everybody and their brother would come in, assume they were good to go, and land!"

So Lonesome Dove's own Hueys and Cobras would often simply forget about making proper approaches. "If they saw a parking space open, they'd just beeline for it," said Capt. Terry "Reverend" Shepherd of the 775.

"You'd have three birds goin' in—first come, first served—fully armed, at night, on night vision goggles, with plane captains just running! If you went to the runway, you'd lose your spot, so you landed right in the spot."

So you can imagine the uproar when the 51 helos came throbbing in for landings after the big abort. "Half of those aircraft hadn't ever *been* to Lonesome Dove," said Husty. "And they didn't know where the hell it was!"

"And there was one corporal in the tower," Shepherd recalled. "The flight leader said, *'Roger, fifty-one aircraft in-bound for fuel and landing on three different runways.'*

"All you could hear was, *'Oh shit.'* and the click of the microphone being dropped in the tower."

Then Husty continued. "When the first aircraft started coming in,

162

landing in all these different directions, I got on the Bat-phone to Command and Control and told them things were fucked up, and that they'd better get control of the tower. The Marine Air Group's CO went over there and saw what the hell was going on.

"This young corporal was overwhelmed," said Husty. "He'd lost total situation awareness. Even an *experienced* tower operator could

All you could hear was, "Oh shit," and the click of the microphone being dropped in the tower.

have had no control over that! They were coming in from every direction, lights on, lights off, trying to hit any spot they could, and didn't know where they were going."

"Then one of our biggest birds, a 53, landed," Shepherd said. "They had a hard landing and put the sconces through the underneath and broke bones of the troops. The ambulances were driving all over the base trying to find them, and all they heard was, 'No, no! They're not over here! You got the wrong spot!'

"And all these birds were fully armed or loaded up with troops or vehicles," Shepherd explained.

"Maintenance Control got a new designation," added Husty. "It became 'Confusion Control.'"

For it's Tommy this, an' Tommy that,

an' "Chuck 'im out, the Brute!"
But it's, "Savior of 'is Country"
When the guns begin to shoot.

Rudyard Kipling

From the scruffiest sappers to the elite Desert Rats, the Brits fielded a force as fearsome as any in the Gulf. And no American I encountered over there ever for a moment doubted British resolve.

But what really intrigued our troops about the Brits was the fact that they were so damned *British*, particularly in their steely, professional cool under fire and in their biting sense of humor. Col. Dick Cody remembered one incident where the British cool was tested:

> We ran into the Brits on the airwaves, during the first attack on the 17th of January. It took us about eight hours to get back from the mission, and all the way we were listening to them, using all their English phrases. I can remember one Brit pilot whose wingman was shot down. He was on-line to AWACS, saying, "I've lost my wingman. We're in a real sticky wicket here." He was *very* calm.

If anyone in the Gulf took issue with the Brits, it was their own. While strolling through the streets of Dharan one night, I ran across some sappers from the 1st Scots Guards. I asked them if they'd seen any humorous incidents during their thrust into Kuwait. With that, they began recounting the tale of a lost Warrior tank which belonged to the famous Desert Rats—or, as the Scots referred to them, the "Desert Hamsters."

The Warrior had become separated from the main column, when suddenly it was surrounded by numerous Soviet-built T-55s. According to the Scots, the Warrior crewmen were shaking in their boots, assuming they bloody well had had it! Then, to their amazement, the T-55s rolled right on by, with fellow coalition members, Egyptians, standing tall in the turrets, flashing victory signs to the Brits.

165

Later I asked Capt. "Lord Lucan" Swinhoe-Standen of the 14th Field Regiment, Royal Artillery, if he could verify this story. Swinhoe-Standen said he couldn't. And, though usually a very funny guy, he found nothing humorous in the 1st Scots' story. But the captain's aide, Bombardier "Fitz" Fitzpatrick, a comic in his own right, did explain why his captain was nicknamed "Lord Lucan." It seems the real Lord Lucan was an English nobleman who disappeared one day, never to be seen again. His Captain, said Fitzpatrick, also disappeared. Frequently. Usually just when he was most needed.

A prize example of British humor, one that bordered comically on insubordination, was told to me by Corporal Paul Goodall, of the mine-clearing 2nd Flail Troop, 16th Squadron, 25th English Regiment:

> The main man came around to my tent once to give us a briefin', an' 'e didn't fetch 'is 'elmet with 'im. When he left, he picked *my* 'elmet up, and walked off with it.
> So the next mornin', I 'ad to go see 'im an' report that my 'elmet 'ad gone up missin'. He said we were goin' to move into the desert *that* day, so it was essential I found it, or I'd probably 'ave my 'ead shot off. And a 'efty fine. So I searched everywhere, for one-and-a-half 'ours, and I was absolutely sweatin'!
> Meanwhile, one of the lads let on talkin' to 'im, "Ah, sir! I know where Corporal Goodall's 'elmet is!"
> "Oh, really? Where's that?" he went.
> "It's on your fuckin' 'ead!"
> "Oh, dear me!" he said.

The British officers were gentlemen, of course, but that never kept them from exchanging humorous digs with their witty insubordinates—even if it was on the wall of a Brit shitter. That's where the following was found. Wrote the first soldier:

> *I'm a 37£ per day Signals Corporal!*
> *What are you infantrymen?*

Wrote the second, who guarded the first:

> *37£-a-day won't keep you alive out here!*

Wrote the CO to both:

> *Well, I'm a 98£-a-day Lt. Colonel,*
> *so SCREW THE LOT OF YOU!*

While I'm on graffiti, here's an example of typical British "black

The Soviet-built T-55s rolled right by with fellow coalition members flashing victory signs to the Brits.

squatty humor," referring to a rumored Gulf War pay raise of 12%—twice the normal 6% rate:

> *Did you hear the gov'ment has awarded us a 12% pay raise?*
> *But, in fact, it will only be 6%, because only half of us will be coming back!*

Speaking of the government, here's another:

> *What is the difference between Margaret Thatcher and Saddam Hussein?*
> *We may yet have a meaningful discussion with Saddam!*

Even when confronted by something as serious as terrorism, the

Brits responded with humor. As did Major Malcolm McKinley, of the 1st UK Armored Division, in his reply to the concerns of an MP:

> There was a very pleasant young officer in the Military Police—which is quite strange because MPs are not normally pleasant—who was clearly very concerned about terrorists. Let's just call him "Lieutenant David."
>
> Lieutenant David rang me one night and said, "Sir, I'm very worried. We've heard about an increase in the terrorist threat. We need some help, and I'd like your advice."
>
> I asked, "David, do you have a 9mm Browning pistol?"
>
> "Yes, sir!" he said.
>
> "You got some bullets?"
>
> "Yes, sir!" he said.
>
> "Well, put them in the pistol," I said. "I'm sorry to be so unhelpful, but I can't think of anything else."

When the Brits crossed paths with the Americans, their humor really hit its stride. Take the time Doc William Smith, of the 511th Tactical Fighter Squadron, hitched a ride north in a Brit helo on what he supposed would be a non-combatant mission:

> We were going to fly a few medical evacuation missions with the Brits from King Khalid Military City. But they bolted this big machine gun beside the door of the helicoper. I said, "Wait a minute. I thought this was a *medical* mission!"
>
> A Brit crewman cocked it and said, "Well, it is—but we want to carry some *medical insurance.*"

Doc Smith wasn't exactly throwing his Geneva convention card out the window, but he was a little concerned!

In addition to the Brits' professionalism and good humor, there was another reason our troops held them in such high regard—the Brits were traders. Whenever American and British convoys passed on desert backroads, they'd pull alongside each other so all their vehicles were lined up abreast. Then they'd set up what amounted to a Gulf War version of a hometown swap meet. The troops from both armies would jump down from the tanks, trucks and lorries, and begin bartering for whatever the other guys wore or carried.

Usually, both armies went away from these affairs happy with their trades. But Captain Kostecki gave me his account of a time when the Brits got the best of his 8th Tankers:

> The sergeant-major of the British squadron had pulled up to the side of the road and was checking one of his tanks that was down. We started talkin' to him.

The troops from both armies would jump from the tanks, trucks and lorries and barter for whatever the other guys wore or carried.

He wanted one of those black and green "ninja jacket" parkas that are designed to hide you at night. He asked me what I wanted for mine.

I asked him, "Well, what do you have?"

"Want a Kevlar helmet?" he asked.

"Nah," I said, "I'm tryin' to get rid of *mine.*"

He said his driver had four berets. I said, "Four berets and a T-shirt, and you got yourself a jacket."

So I pointed him over to my tank, but before *I* got there, he'd traded Sergeant Murray an old, ratty T-shirt for *his* parka.

I asked Sergeant Murray, "Did you get your four berets?"

"What four berets?" he said.

Just then the sergeant-major went by. He already had his jacket on, and he waved to us as he drove away.

Parkas, berets, and T-shirts weren't the only things swapped between the Americans and Brits. They also swapped jokes—often the practical variety. Like the time the Brits pulled a good one on the 6th Marines' (2 MARDIV) trackers. The AAVs must have expected just another swapfest when they spotted the Brits heading their way. But according to one grunt, that's not what they got:

> We were makin' a movement about ninety miles north, and the Brits saw us coming, so they decided they'd play a little joke. They put their MOPP suits on. Our major saw them and went hysterical. He hollered, *"MOPP LEVEL 4! Gas! Gas!"*
> Everybody started running around the TRAK, scramblin' to get into MOPP suits. SSgt. Huggart was just sittin' around on the vehicle with only his gas mask on, saying, "It's only a drill! Take it easy! It's only a drill!"
> Captain Whittaker turned around and—BOOM!—hit Huggart right in the face with a MOPP suit and screamed, *"We don't drill in MOPP Level 4!"*
> "Really?" Huggart croaked.
> The whole company threw their gas suits on. The Brits just *loved* it!

Even when the Americans received the short end of the stick—as often they did—they still delighted in the British gift for having fun.

But the Americans weren't the only ones to feel British barbs. The French have always provided the Brits with a rich array of targets for humor. And the Brits have generally been happy to oblige.

So it was during Desert Storm, when the French were assigned the task of making a feint far to the west. The idea was to fool Saddam into holding some of his forces in the Bagdad area. The feint worked. But the fact that the French were out of sight for most of the war gave the Brits all the reason they needed to poke fun in their direction.

As IV Brigade's armor raced north into Kuwait, one Brit tanker hollered to another, "Where are the French?"

"They're getting ready for dinner!" his mate yelled back.

All jokes aside, the coalition forces, including the French, were very grateful that the Brits had joined them in the Gulf War and didn't just sit it out like the Swiss, who—as a Swiss reporter in Kuwait City explained—declined to fight because "it was very dangerous and it cost money."

"We are a down-to-earth people," the reporter added.

Good thing the British aren't.

Getting Lost

You went to the muffler and took a left.

Sgt. Frank Lahue
2nd Marines, 2 MARDIV

To me, Master Gunnery Sergeant Larry Kennedy was the epitome of the Marine Corps gunny. He'd been everywhere and seen everything. He looked like an old battle vet marine was *supposed* to look, and he knew his stuff.

But even Master Gunny Kennedy was blown out when it came to navigating around the flat, barren, featureless terrain of the Arabian Peninsula. And the military maps he was issued didn't help much. If anything, they depicted the terrain *too* accurately.

"They had about 47 map sheets to get us from Saudi to our objective," Kennedy told me. "And every one of them looked the same—they were just brown. The only variance on them was their blue grid lines."

Incredible as it may seem, the troops were sometimes better off when they ignored their maps and trusted instead in their instinctual sense of distance and direction. Other times, just having a map—any map—was good enough, as Capt. "Franco" Francavilla of the Army's 1st Cavalry Division discovered:

> When Colonel Parker was navigating, he somehow *always* found the right place. We all wondered, "How does he read a map? There's nothing here! No hills, no valleys, no streams..."
>
> The S-2 said, "Hey, sir. Can I see your map?" He took it and looked at it, and it was the *wrong* map! It was a completely different area, but he'd been using that map and following it!
>
> So we just started using any map in the world, renumbering as necessary.

Even in the established, heavily travelled areas, people frequently got lost. What few roads there were in those deserts had few if any road signs. So the troops usually had to find their way with

*You had enough trouble worrying about where
the empty oil drum was, or the two tires stacked
on top of each other—the road markers.*

the help of impromptu reference points, which meant anything available that was in some respect distinctive. Gunny Kennedy elaborated:

> When you went somewhere, you followed the same tracks every time. If you moved off the beaten path, you'd create a whole new road. You had enough trouble worrying about where the empty oil drum was, or the two tires stacked on top of each other, or the three empty cases of food rations—the *road markers*. So, to get off the road from Camp 15, you made the right-hand turn at the burned-out school bus.

"And then somebody would drive by and move them on you," added SSgt. Raymond Howard. "If they moved them to the other side of the road, then you were really in a trick. Ten miles down the road you'd realize, *'That wasn't right!'"*

On missions during the Ground War, a Global Plotting System (GPS) was often employed as a guide for field operations. This satellite system kept the troops on track when they couldn't navigate using the terrain.

But the GPS wasn't practical for everyday use—for running errands, ferrying supplies, or scouting for souvenirs. Sometimes even tactical convoys wouldn't use it, if the right link-up equipment wasn't available.

Still, with someone like Colonel Parker, it really didn't matter what methods were at hand, because he always found his way. And it's doubtful it would have mattered much, either, to someone like a certain sergeant from the 43rd Engineers, 3rd ACR, who always got himself lost. PFC Brian Bess told me about his sergeant:

> It seemed like whenever my platoon sergeant went somewhere he got lost, but he never admitted it. And he *refused* to stop and ask for directions.
>
> When our platoon was coming back from Iraq, he was leading us. It was supposed to be a 150-160 mile trip. It should've taken us one day at the speed we were going. The next thing we knew, we were all seeing things we'd never seen before.
>
> We drove through some Brits.
> We drove through 24th ID.
> We drove through 3rd ACR.
> We drove through VII Corps.
>
> By the time we got where we were going, we'd driven over 465 miles out of our way!
>
> When he finally got there, we kept sayin' he was lost, and he kept sayin', "I wasn't lost! I just didn't know where we were going!"

The Convoy to Hell

There were also those times, in navigating the vast Arabian Peninsula, when it wasn't his direction a soldier would lose, but his mind. Riding in a desert convoy was probably one of the easiest ways to lose both.

After interminable hours of droning down Saudi highways, or jolting along Bedouin camel trails, mesmerized by the humming tires or the creaks and rattles, expressions would turn sullen, tempers would grow short, and reality would become meaningless.

So it went on the "Convoy to Hell," the 595th Medical Company's excursion into lunacy. Sgt. Michael Malloy got the tale underway:

I'll never forget the day. We were in the back of an Army 2 1/2–ton truck, about fifteen of us, with our gear strewn all over the place, somewhere in southern Iraq. We were in our third day.

Bodies were funking bad. Tensions were flaring. And...dust was rising. (There's always *three* things.)

We stopped at about two o'clock in the morning. People had been in the back for about seven hours. The order was given: "Nobody get out of the vehicle! There's land mines!"

Soldiers, stammering to try to take a piss, couldn't get out. Out came the empty plastic water bottles. They were everywhere.

There was one female in the crowd. Her name was Rogers. She was crying, "What should I do?"

Well, she did what any red-blooded American girl would do when her bladder was full. *"Guy-y-ys! We need to make a stop!"*

She hung off the side of the tail-gate while Specialist Wonder put a blanket over her, so we couldn't see the front of her—but the rest of Iraq could see the back of her!

We finally pulled up to our site, after about fourteen hours of riding. Nobody seemed to know where we were going, and we made a horseshoe formation of all the vehicles.

We were sitting there, ready to set our tents up, when the order was given to move again. So we clambered back into our vehicles. This time tensions were flaring even hotter. The gear was worse than ever. The people had been

He keeps his eyes open like a shark, even when he's asleep. He drives like a zombie.

eating MREs for almost a week, so there was a lot of exchanges of gas—and a high concentration of farts in the back of the truck.

Later, a little farther north, the 595th pulled up for the night. But there wasn't much time to rest from the rigors of the road. As Sergeant Malloy remembered, they spent the time sharpening the skills that were sure to be needed when they hit the front lines:

We were taking mock casualty patients all night long. It was really taxing our abilities.
Once again, the tensions were flaring.
At about four o'clock in the morning, we had only a skeleton crew on, and they had just got done taking care of about thirty patients. When—BAM!—came another twenty patients, dropped on our doorstep.
Some "lost" second lieutenant came running up and

said, "Doc! I got casualties for you! All kinds! They're in serious trouble!"

Being the good medic that I was, and though I hadn't slept for twenty-four hours, I went running into the sleep tent and said, *"We got another twenty fucking casualties!"*

I woke the whole crowd up and we got ready to treat the casualties. I asked the lieutenant what was wrong with them.

And he said, "Well, they're all dead!"

Well, you can imagine the turmoil and the torment after that. Everybody nuked me for waking them up.

Then it was back on the road again. The wear and tear of this seemingly endless ride into madness stressed the 595th to its limits. Eventually, as Sgt. David Hebert explained, the strain began to take its toll:

For twenty-two hours it was stop and go. On the eighteenth hour, we'd stopped for about twenty minutes. Lieutenant Butler and I were the lead vehicle, and, when we started taking off, all the vehicles behind us still stayed there. We couldn't understand.

Then we realized that they might have been sleeping or something, so Lieutenant Butler decided to go out and get 'em moving.

He went up to Specialist Burhans' truck and found him dead asleep. Lieutenant Butler opened the door and said, "All right. You gotta switch drivers! You're tired."

And Specialist Burhans swore up and down, *"I'm following ya! I'm following ya!"*

According to Lieutenant Butler, Burhans wasn't even reclining in his seat, he was sleeping while sitting straight up.

"He was in the fifth truck that I went to," said Butler. "The first five driver teams were *all* asleep!"

So, the lieutenant woke them, and the convoy rolled on. Butler told me how he'd always been happy to ride with Sergeant Hebert, "because he kinda likes to do the 'stud' thing and drive it all by himself."

"After about sixteen or eighteen hours—a very valiant effort," said Butler, "he starts to fall asleep. But he keeps his eyes open like a shark, even when he's asleep. He drives like a zombie. If you're awake yourself, you look over to see if he's okay. You say, 'Sergeant Hebert, how you doing?'

"*I'm fine! I'm fine!*' That's usually when he comes up with his best quips and quotes," chuckled Butler, "like the memorable, 'Anthrax sticks to kids.'"

The lieutenant woke them all, and the convoy rolled on. But somewhere in mid-journey, something finally snapped. Dr. Howard Heidenberg, one of the victims, recalled that point in the journey:

> Most of us were pretty nervous, pretty sure that the land mines were clear but not *totally* sure of it. And most of us got *really* scared when mortar fire started coming in. It was treacherous there. We were the lead vehicle, combing the way.
>
> Suddenly, the middle of our convoy was hit. I think some of the people in our vehicle were hit, too. I immediately jumped out and, applying the principles and techniques of advance life support, I patched up three soldiers, while forming a one-man perimeter, firing my M-45 with my left hand, then going automatic with my M-16.
>
> I was a fairly accurate shot, though I'm right-handed. I'm not exactly sure how many Iraqis I took out, but it was a large number, considering I had two entire clips of tracer rounds.
>
> I guess the best part about it was that all the allies lived. I carried them back to the cucvee, which I converted into an OR. I then utilized Major Cardinal, Sergeant Hebert, and Lieutenant Butler as my assistants and anesthesiologist, respectively. Basically, everyone lived, and we continued on without losing a beat in the convoy.
>
> But, that's just sort of my own personal story. Or what I used to *dream* about, anyway.

After 22 hours, the 595th arrived at its destination in southern Iraq. But, as they hit the ground, the word came—*The war was over!*

"Twenty-two hours of driving for nothing?" Captain Heidenberg asked Sergeant Hebert. Then he said, "Let's go find some EPWs to work on!"

As the troops began to set up their tents, Sergeant Malloy looked around him, astonished and disconcerted. This wasn't what they were expecting. "We were looking for enemies and casualties," said Malloy, "and, well, they just weren't there.

"As far as we were concerned," Malloy concluded, "it was just another training exercise of the 595th Medical Company (Clearing)."

Sniper!

From the outset of the Gulf deployment, the terrorist threat was a big concern for our military leaders. Nobody wanted a repeat of the Beruit barracks bombing.

But many troops either downplayed the threat or simply ignored it, probably figuring that no such thing could happen to *them*. Such was the case with one marine I met in Al Jubail. Having spent considerable time searching enemy bunkers, and viewing the "porn" that they contained, he asked me with a broad grin, "What's everybody so afraid of?—That some Iraqi's gonna bust in here and *flash* us?"

Still, no matter how much the troops tried to ignore it, a vague fear of terrorism lingered inside of everyone. After all, with that many Americans in the Middle East, and Saddam calling for Muslim holy war, wasn't there bound to be at least some terrorist attempt now and then?

Often, all it would take to turn the troops' subliminal fear into full-blown panic was a car backfiring, the crash of a falling metal object, or an accidental discharge. Given this, then, the stage was set for the "Airport Sniper."

It happened one early January evening, in Al Jubail Airport's tent city. Marine Capt. Verne Seaton, from the HML-767 Nomads, gave me his account:

> It was about two weeks after we'd got into Saudi. There were four or five of us in our tent. One of the guys had just gone out to fill up a canteen at the water buffalo—when we heard a pistol shot!
>
> It was dark, probably around 19:30. The shot went off, and people started to yell, *"Everybody down! Freeze!"*
>
> A couple seconds later, Dell Forth came busting in with Larry O'Neil right behind him. Both of them were panic-struck, telling us frantically that there was a gunman out in the compound. Dell yelled, *"Get the lights out!"*
>
> Larry shouted, *"I'll get the back door! Somebody get the front!"*
>
> So we turned off the lights, thinking that there was going to be a rain of bullets coming through the canvas. None of us were ready and we scrambled around in the darkness, trying to find all the stuff that we'd only recently

come to own courtesy of the Marine Corps, but it was all scattered about somewhere the dark. Everyone was yelling, *"Get down!"* but we were all standing straight up, rummaging and thinking, *Where's my flak jacket? I gotta be ready for this!*

We all had flashlights and pistols drawn, waiting for those gunmen in the compound.

Then two or three people got on the back door, and two or three got on the front, and we all had flashlights and pistols drawn, waiting for those gunmen in the compound.

Suddenly, one person said, "I'm gonna chamber a round." And we heard the slide go—*clk!*

There was a couple seconds of silence, as everyone thought to themselves, *Hey. That's a good idea...*

Clk-clk! Clk-clk, clk!

Then, after a few minutes, someone gave the "all clear." It turned out that somebody had been cleaning their pistol, but not quite in line with Marine Corps orders!

After I'd heard Seaton's account, I wandered over to the squadron's flight ops trailer, and sat around having coffee with several senior enlisted people. One of them, Gunny Michael T. Allen, gave me a little more background on the "sniper" incident:

> We had a young lieutenant cleaning his weapon and he accidentally fired off a round. Everybody yelled out that there was a sniper shootin' in the camp.
>
> That round went over ten different tents in ten different directions. Everybody swears that round went right over their head!
>
> People in the showers said, *"It came right by here!"*
>
> Ten feet in the other direction, somebody said, *"It went right by my head!"*
>
> It was a ricochet round, I guess!

Though the "sniper" incident proved to be nothing but a false alarm, it certainly raised the alert level of the average troop. They were never quite as lackadaisical as they had been before. The next time a round was fired, it could be *real*—and they wouldn't be caught off-guard again.

But the heightened alert status also triggered a certain amount of paranoia, as Coyote CO Lt. Col. "Pablo" Martin discovered to his amusement:

> Our flight surgeon is probably one of the smartest guys in the world, but he's got a lot of personality quirks. One of the things he does is get these nightmares in the middle of the night. And at the top of his lungs, he starts screaming, *"Ah! Aaaagh. AAAAAAAAAAAGH!"*
>
> It's not one of those things you want to hear in the middle of a SCUD attack, you know? I mean, you don't know if there's bad guys coming into the tent or what!
>
> So, one of the other pilots was sound asleep, and suddenly he heard the flight surgeon yelling, "AAAGH!" So he woke up, and saw this black image in front of him.
>
> Well, the black image was his flight suit, which he'd hung up next to his bed. But *he* didn't know that. He started kicking the black image in the balls! He was attacking his flight suit, thinking there were bad guys in the tent coming to get him!

Another example of caution breeding paranoia involved a long bus ride some of the HMA-775 guys took to war. Coyote Capt. Terry "Reverend" Shepherd remembered it well:

> The ultimate insanity was taking a bus to go to war.

Our bus was a perfect terrorist target. Everybody was locked and cocked, their weapons pointing out the window.

There were forty-five marines all in combat gear, flak jackets, and helmets. You couldn't chamber a round 'til you were off the base, but everybody was going, *Please. Please take a shot. Just make an attempt to get us!*

And as soon as that bus left, you heard every bolt slam onto the rounds, everybody thinking, *Come on! I want five terrorists just to make a shot!*

Later we were going along at eleven o'clock at night, and the bus died! Everybody instantly thought, *Okay, this is our chance! They must've sabotaged the bus, and now they're waitin' here to ambush us!*

Everybody jumped out and deployed!

I could just see a helicopter flying by. And here's thirty marines below it, laying out in the dirt, deployed alongside this road, next to this stupid, broken-down bus that nobody gives crap about—all thinking, *Come on, ple-e-ase!* And they're all air wingers!

Chicken Colonels

Saddam's threat to use deadly gases in the Gulf was the war's true common denominator, because, if there were a gas attack, *everyone* would be targeted—rank would hold no privilege.

So, throughout the theater, all troops of all ranks were issued gas

***None of these officers had their masks, and they
were all scrambling to find them.***

masks and protective clothing, and ordered to keep them with their persons at all times. And when an attack came, everyone was expected to cover his or her own ass with his or her own gear. Rarely would there be extras laying around with "For Any Serviceman" labels attached.

But, in war, orders and expectations sometimes go awry—as they did with HQ Bn., 2 MARDIV, on the last day of the war just outside

Kuwait City. SSgt. Brian Jones, who was assigned to one of Division's NBC (nuclear-biological-chemical) vehicles, gave me this account:

I don't know exactly where on the map it was. It was a place everybody called "Hell." We were heading toward Kuwait International Airport, when we stopped.

It was about noon, but the smoke from the oil wells came over us and it was just like midnight. All of the battalion commanders from the TAC force came around the regimental CO for a meeting.

Suddenly, an arty shell impacted somewhere in the area. Everybody looked up and decided it might be gas, and started scrambling for their gas masks.

All of these officers had always cautioned the other marines about keeping their masks with them at all times, but it turned out none of *them* had their masks, and they were all scrambling and running across to different vehicles trying to find them.

The ones who'd brought their masks with them and had laid them down on the ground were fighting over them. Everybody was trying to say that it was his mask.

I saw a couple of officers tugging on one mask. One of them was saying it was *his*, and the other one was saying it was *his*.

And it was a pretty comical situation, because there must've been probably twenty to twenty-five officers—majors, lieutenant colonels, colonels, first sergeants, sergeant majors—all the heavy hitters! It looked like just a big gaggle, everybody fightin' over masks and running to get theirs.

We were sitting up in the FOX vehicle, in overpressure, and we couldn't do anything but laugh!

A Doc for All Seasons

Like all the wars before it, Desert Storm had its share of heroes, and they revealed themselves in most of the traditional categories.

There were the *dubious* heroes, those who were definitely heroic, but under suspect circumstances. Such as the Army command sergeant-major who—too high in rank to be given his own M1-A1—"borrowed" a spare Abrams and freelanced about, killing Iraqi tanks and taking numbers.

There were the *accidental* heroes, those driven unwittingly by quirks of fate into acts of valor. Like the two marines from the 2 MARDIV who were inadvertently locked out of their armored amphib vehicle (AAV) in the face of enemy fire. They swung around the AAV's 50-caliber machine gun and blasted away at the Iraqis till they had earned themselves a couple of Bronze Stars.

And, of course, there were the *"real"* heroes: the fighter and bomber pilots who flung themselves with abandon against the Iraqi AAA defenses; the tankers who busted through the Iraqi "line of death" and blazed their way to the gates of Kuwait City; and the MEDEVAC aviators who flew countless unarmed sorties into hostile territory to rescue fallen comrades.

Then, there were the *unsung* heroes who were as real as any, but less recognized for their deeds. They, too, laid it all on the line, only in relative obscurity. Such a hero was Doc Prestine.

Six years before the Gulf War, Col. Arthur P. Prestine thought his military career was over. He'd suffered a massive heart attack that forced him to retire from his cherished position as anesthesiologist, or "ether bunny." After almost two years of military retirement, however, Doc Prestine was so bored he began a small general practice in Buffalo, New York.

When Saddam invaded Kuwait, Doc went back to his old unit to volunteer for overseas duty. "But my dear friend the commander, Richard Hopkins, felt that he didn't want me to die in the sand," Doc explained to me. "And I think he was right. However, I screamed bloody murder until somebody heard my pleas."

The 800th Military Police Brigade, an Army Reserve outfit in New York, welcomed him aboard, and, with the 800th, Doc deployed to Saudi as a brigade surgeon.

Of all the characteristics attributed to human beings, the one most prevalent in Doc was his empathy. Doc Prestine genuinely cared about people and he spent his Gulf War tour proving it.

Doc's primary job with the 800th was to oversee the health care and general welfare of the theater's 7500 MPs and tens of thousands of Enemy Prisoners of War (EPWs).

But he took on another job, too—that of a highly mobile emergency room doctor. As he rode along the deadly Saudi highways, from one EPW camp to another, Doc kept alert for any serious traffic accidents where he could be of help. His driver and bodyguard, Sgt. Michael "The Brooklyn Brute" Bitando, described one accident scene he'll never forget, and Doc's instinctual response to it:

> I was comin' back from the north camp with Colonel Prestine. We were on Tapline Road, where more people have gotten killed than in the war.
>
> This tank accident was probably the most horrifying thing I've ever seen. It consisted of two tractor-trailers, one carrying an M-1 tank and one with Egyptian and Saudi soldiers aboard. When we arrived on the scene, there were people actually cut in half and crushed into the wreckage.
>
> Colonel Prestine, without worrying about his own life, climbed onto the truck and into the wreckage to save these people's lives. With fuel spilling all over the place, I had to use force to pull Col. Prestine off of the truck. The thing could have exploded at any time.
>
> Colonel Prestine stood there helplessly. There was nothing he could do. Everyone was dead. We just felt helpless being there.

Doc's concern for others always overrode any fears for his own safety, certainly a basic tenant in anyone's definition of heroism. Sergeant Bitando remembered another of the Doc's highway mercy missions, this one involving civilians:

> There were many other times we were on the road when we were unable to save people's lives. Last week, we came upon a crushed Saudi car with four children trapped inside. Colonel Prestine started *five* IVs. But yesterday, when we went up to King Fahd Medical Center, we learned that one little girl had died that night.

In addition to his boundless empathy, Doc Prestine had an insatiable curiosity, which also produced many unforgettable moments—though most of these had a humorous touch, such as the time he won over a bunch of Iraqi EPWs. Doc told me this one himself:

> On the 18th of March, as a part of my job, I was in the prison camps and I particularly wanted to talk to the

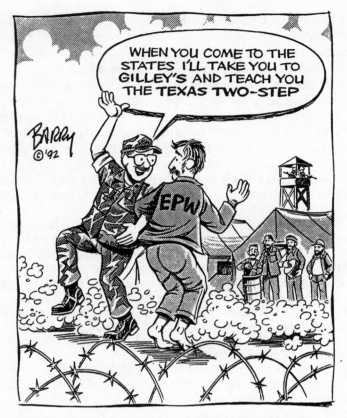

I couldn't resist! I went inside the enclosure and started dancing with the EPWs.

Enemy Prisoner of War physicians. We'd captured quite a number of them, about thirty-five or forty, and I just wanted to ask them how they felt the medical care was, and if they were satisfied or had any ideas on how we could improve it. They all said the medical care was very good, which made me very happy.

I walked over to the concertina wire fence, and asked the EPWs, "Do you guys know how to dance?" So they got an English-speaking EPW, and I told him, "I would like to see an Iraqi dance. Can you help me?"

He gathered up about two hundred EPWs, and had them all sit down and the ones in the back stand up. He made a three-quarter circle, so there was an opening where Sergeant Bitando and I could watch.

It was the damnedest thing I ever saw in my life. They got a five-gallon drum, a big tin can—and I don't know what else they were using for instruments—but they started playing music with their fingers. They all started clapping and singing what I remember as a "beaver sound," like this, *"Hiebebebubababebebabe!"*

I'd heard that sound in Morocco; I wasn't sure what the indication of it was. But they started dancing around, and clapping, and singing, and yelling. Some EPWs jumped up on others' shoulders and they danced around in a circle together.

As luck would have it, I recognized one dance the Lebanese call the Dubk, which I used to be able to do, myself.

I couldn't resist! I went inside the enclosure and started dancing with the EPWs. And then they really went wild! The guards up in their towers thought there was a riot going on, I'm sure!

It kept up for about twenty minutes, and they all cheered and clapped, and I was unbelievably happy.

Doc Prestine often invited EPWs to visit him in his New York home once the war was over. And he'd give them things, as tokens of his friendship. Once, he gave away something that he himself really treasured:

I met an EPW who was an infantry lieutenant named Jesim. We struck up a friendship, and I used to talk with him at length.

I've actually invited him to visit me in Buffalo, and we're working on that deal.

Shortly after the Super Bowl, a friend of mine sent me a white Super Bowl cap with the Bills and the Giants on it. Although I really liked the cap, I felt it was most appropriate to give it to my EPW acquaintance, Jesim.

So here's an EPW walking around a prison camp with a Super Bowl cap on, less than two weeks after the Super Bowl. Obviously, the GIs were astounded!

"This is the enemy?"

MEMORANDUM STO-5000-05-30E

UNDERSTANDING YOUR ENEMY

Item One: To fulfill his duty to Saddam, an Iraqi
soldier must first fire one clip from an AK-47
into the air, then he can wave a white flag.

Item Two: The new Iraqi flag is a white crescent
moon on a white background.

Item Three: Part of the Iraqi soldier's uniform
is a pair of white undershorts, so if he wants
to surrender, but has no new Iraqi flag, all he
has to do is take off his shorts and wave them
around.

Throughout my travels in the Gulf, I kept an ear open for wild and weird tales. And whenever I raised the subject of Enemy Prisoners of War I always got an earful.

I figure it was partly because so many of our troops had personal contact with the EPWs. There certainly were enough prisoners to go around, as suggested by the joke: "I hear Saddam Hussein used to have the *fourth* largest army in the world—but now he has the *second* largest army in Saudi Arabia."

You didn't even have to be a frontline warrior to rub elbows with captured Iraqis. You could have been part of a helo MEDEVAC crew, transporting wounded EPWs to rear echelon hospitals, or patched-up prisoners from the hospitals to EPW camps. Or have served on the medical staff at one of those hospitals, or visited a "friendly" patient there when enemy casualties checked in. Or you could have worked as support personnel at one of the prison camps, as a computer clerk or an interpreter, an engineer or an MP. But, all in all, the best stuff I collected did come from the guys and gals up front, like the story about a certain Army motor transport sergeant.

The sergeant was on just another uneventful mission in an endless string of missions ferrying men and supplies to the front. Suddenly, out of nowhere, 21 Iraqi soldiers ran onto the road ahead.

Their hands were raised in surrender, and they were waving white sheets, towels, and undershorts.

The driver ground the big rig to a halt, grabbed an M-16 carbine off the seat, and jumped out. Checking the Iraqis closely for weapons and being satisfied they were unarmed and quite sincere about surrendering, the sergeant directed them up into the bed of the 2 1/2–ton rig, tossing them bottled water and MREs as they boarded.

Then the driver took off her helmet, shook her hair loose, and climbed back into the cab of the truck. All at once a chorus of wails rose from the prisoners.

"Woman! Woman!" they cried, realizing to their horror that they had just given up to a female. And one by one they dismounted and started hoofing it down the road, apparently to find some American male to take them in.

But this truck-driving female was not buying the Arab concept of a woman's lot in life. She leaped down from the cab again and sprayed the air above the departing Iraqis with her M-16. Instantly they dove for the sand, once more gesturing their desire to surrender.

Later that day, the sergeant pulled into camp with her EPWs. The company CO, amazed by the sight of her unlikely cargo, strode over to check it out.

One of the Iraqis turned to the American captain and, jabbing his finger in the direction of the driver, hollered in his limited English, *"Mean woman!"*

Probably the best publicized EPW incident involved the Iraqi-American college student who had returned to Bagdad on vacation—just before the war. When Saddam invaded Kuwait, this young man was "enlisted" in the Iraqi army.

Months later, after suffering the horrors of hunger, thirst, and B-52 raids, he was surrounded by some U.S. Marines. Imagine the look on the marines' faces as he jumped out of his bunker, still in his Yale T-shirt and shorts, and ran to greet them yelling, *"WHERE THE HELL HAVE YOU GUYS BEEN?"*

Most of the troops in the Gulf knew of this incident. They'd either read it in the newspaper or heard about it from someone who had.

Another bizarre EPW encounter also received a lot of publicity. It involved a Marine vehicle that was mired in a mudhole. The oddest thing about this story was the way it changed with every telling. It had more variations than Saddam had rotten ideas.

The first and simplest version was given to me by Sgt. Ernie Grafton of the HQ Bn., 2 MARDIV:

> There was a humvee stuck in the mud. A BMP started moving on them. It's a small Soviet anti-personnel carrier,

with eight men in the back. This thing sports a .25mm gun.

Our guys fired two rounds out of a rifle at this thing, and the Iraqis came out and surrendered. The marines thought, "Son of a *bitch!*"

From Ernie's basic account, the story grew more and more embellished. Pretty soon there was only one marine in the hummer. And he was pulled out of the mud by a tank before the Iraqis surrendered. "Just one marine with an M-16 against a tank!" was how another marine put it. Then the marine became an army first sergeant and the "tank" became a T-72 *and* a BMP—but the Iraqis were *still* surrendering.

Though both the "Kid from Chicago" and the "Stuck Humvee" episodes circulated widely in country, there were numerous others— equally off-the-wall—that didn't. I've included several of them for your enjoyment below:

SFC Curtis Roderick, 4th Marines, 2 MARDIV:
The Echo Company's XO had captured these fifteen Iraqis, tied them up, and left them on the side of the road. We got three or four miles down the road, when Maj. Van Fleet said for us to go back and cut them loose.

So we drove back to them to cut them loose. Now, these guys were *scared.* First of all, they'd been shot up by a tank with a machine gun. Then a sniper with .50 cal had shot a round through one of their fighting holes. Next they had watched an entire battalion of Marine infantry go through, plus a company of M1-A1 tanks, plus a regimental logistics train, plus a combat train—all this firepower go through in front of their eyes.

And here we came, driving back in a couple of humvees. We pulled up and got out, looking bigger than we actually were, because of our flak jackets, helmets, and guns.

They looked at us like, "Well? What are you guys here for?"

I walked over and pulled my K-bar [knife] out and fingered it, to see if it was sharp enough to cut the ropes.

The next thing I knew, they were looking at me like, *"My god!"*

But we just cut them loose one at a time, gave them some water and food, ham slices or some shit like that. Then they wanted cigarettes!

We decided we weren't gonna do any more for them. They sat around in a circle, and, suddenly, some *fool* came driving by in a humvee with MOPP 4 on. So we put on

*This truck-driving female was not buying
the Arab concept of a woman's lot in life.*

MOPP 4, too—I broke my glasses getting into it! We even taped our wrists. Then we were ready for the mustard gas or whatever it was.

So these Iraqis were thinking, *Number one, this guy almost killed us with a knife. Number two, he probably poisoned us with his water. And number three, now he's gettin' dressed up because we're gonna get gassed by our own people!*

PFC Duane Hendricks, HHC 24th Aviation Bde:
We were sittin' beside an M1. Suddenly this guy jumps out from behind a little sandhill, shoots an RPG at the M1. But it just bounced off. So then he yelled, *"GIVE UP!"* and started waving a white flag.

1st Lt. Mark Eichelman, XO, Alpha Co., 1-67 Tiger Bde:
They wanted us to get up to Kuwait City as fast as

possible, so we weren't stopping to round up prisoners. Yet, as we were rolling through all these bunker complexes, Iraqis ran out waving their white flags, their hands up. We kept on going, and they all looked upset because we weren't stopping to bring them in. They were running behind the tanks, and we were waving them back in the other direction!

Sgt. Scott A. Smith, 4th TOWs, 2 MARDIV:
They had four rows of EPWs, about two hundred of 'em, up on the road behind a five-ton. As far as I could see, there were EPWs in ranks, four of 'em, all on their hands and knees, looking like they'd just gotten through eatin' chow.

Some guy was standing there going, "ONE-TWO-THREE-FOUR!"

And all the Iraqis would say, "UNITED STATES MARINE CORPS! HOO-RAH!"

And then they'd start all over!

SSgt. John Thibideaux, Army Motor Transport:
There were some other guys who had a truckload of EPWs, about fifteen, and they were driving through the desert at night. I guess they wound up going in a big circle, heading in the wrong direction—*north!* The Iraqis started bangin' on the back of the window telling them they were going in the wrong way, and showing them the direction to Saudi Arabia!

Col. Arthur P. "Doc" Prestine, 800th MP Bde:
An MP had his weapon in his hands, and was talking to an EPW, who was showing him pictures of his Iraqi family. So the GI decided to show the guy some pictures of his *own* family in America.

So he handed the guy his M-16 and started reaching for his wallet, then quickly he realized that he'd just given his weapon to an Enemy Prisoner of War.

Capt. Douglas "Tonto" Dry, 4th TOWs, 2 MARDIV:
There were a few Iraqis who made a mistake and fired a weapons system at a few humvees headin' their way. Suddenly, it was like the whole Marine Corps came down on those few Iraqis!

All the marines were itching to get in the war, because they were all afraid that it would be over before they got involved in some battle. So tanks came up and started firing, and by the time they got them shut down, the AAVs were already on their way, and *they* started firing! When

**The MP decided to show the EPW some
pictures of his family in America.**

they finally got one group to quit firing, another group was
on their way because they heard the action.

There were actually only a half a dozen or so Iraqis—
but they were probably all beatin' the *shit* out of the two or
three that had fired at us!

One EPW told our guys that he was just tired of
fightin'. He said, "When we fought all those years against
Iran, the Iranians would run. But when we fought the
Marines, *more of them would come!*"

Master Gunny Larry Kennedy, 4th Marines, 2 MARDIV:
They brought some woman major up here, and she was
looking through all the bunkers. She was off by herself,
and didn't have her pistol with her or anything.

She checked out this one bunker, trying to find some
souvenirs, but didn't find anything.

She looked in another one. Nothing in there.

When she opened the door to the third bunker, there were six Iraqis in there with AK-47s!

One of them said, "American?"

"Yeah," she said.

They handed her their weapons and said, "We surrender!"

I guess they didn't want to get taken by Egyptians or Kuwaitis.

Sgt. Michael Malloy, 595th Medical Company (Clearing):

Late one night, the EPWs were coming in the hospital. One guy was dressed better, looking like a Republican Guard. He was standing there tiredly with an arm injury.

Sgt. "Woodsy" Morris came by with a cot for him. The guy sat down, looked at Woodsy, and thought, *My god. This is the enemy, and the guy gives me a chair?*

They searched him, gave him the POW treatment, and tossed him an MRE. The guy looked at it and didn't know what it was. He opened it up, and it was pork.

One of the guys said, "Pork?"

The Iraqi looked at him.

The guy went, "Oink, oink, squeal, squeal?"

The Republican Guard said, in English, "Shit! I don't care if I'm Islamic or not! I haven't eaten anything in a week! *I'm eating!*"

Doc Prestine:

There was also a female MP guard who was taking some prisoners out on a cleanup detail, to pick up papers around the camp and so forth. They were gonna take a shortcut out of the compound, so she showed them how to lift up a wire so you could crawl under it safely and not be injured—because concertina wire was very sharp. It seemed amusing that an MP would be showing an Iraqi prisoner how to escape through the barbed wire without being injured.

Capt. A. N. Onimas, 8th Tank Bn., 2 MARDIV:

We had about fifty EPWs sitting on the side of the road with their hands bound, when one individual said, "I gotta go to the bathroom!"

So our lance corporal said, "Well, okay. That won't be too bad." And he proceeded to untie him, so the guy could go relieve himself.

Pretty soon, the rest of them were going, *"Hey! Me, too! Me, too!"*

But the lance corporal said, "Well, I'm not gonna untie all these guys just to tie them back up!"

So he made the guy that he'd untied unzip and relieve

all of the fifty Iraqis who had raised their hands and said
they had to take a leak!

Sgt. Ernie Grafton, HQ Bn., 2 MARDIV:
    There was an RPV, a remote-controlled airplane,
circling overhead. And the Iraqis kept following it with
their hands up in the air. They surrendered to a remote
control plane!

PFC Aaron Allen, HHC 24th Aviation Bde:
    We were stopped in a convoy, and we were lost. We
wanted to make sure we were on the right heading, so
Lieutenant Townsend and I were walking along the trucks.
There was a guy bent down by a truck in his BVD's.
Lieutenant Townsend tapped him on the shoulder and
said, "Hey! Is this such and such a place?"
    The guy looked up. He had his mouth gagged and he
was handcuffed. He was an EPW!

Doc Prestine:

On another occasion, an Enemy Prisoner of War escaped from the wire compound that he was held in. He went up to a hamburger stand—what they called a "Roach Coach"—by the general prison site. Well, they gave him a hamburger, and he started to pay for it in Iraqi money. Obviously, they caught on and queried him about his status!

Staff Sergeant Thibideaux:

There were three M1s and a Bradley, chasing an Iraqi soldier with a jeep. He decided the jeep wasn't fast enough, so he got out and started running. They chased him down and he stopped.

They laid him down and started frisking him. The lieutenant was checking him for weapons and everything, and the Iraqi soldier reached around and started *kissing* him. The lieutenant got pretty bent outta shape over that, but that Iraqi just wanted to go to prison.

Sgt. Kenneth Lowry, HHC 24th Army Aviation Bde:

We kept hearing about how everybody was catching EPWs, but we hadn't seen any of them. Then we went across the border and got set up in this position. Some guys in a Bradley pulled up. They had got lost, and they were looking for an EPW area to take the Iraqi that they had in the back.

So about twenty people ran over to look at him, just to see what this guy looked like. We got over there, and the guy was just trembling—you know, like we were gonna kill him or something! He was just scared to death.

And everybody was getting next to him, putting their arm around him, taking pictures. The first thing that came out of his mouth, as he put his thumb in the air, was, *"BUSH! BUSH! NUMBER ONE!"* Then he said, *"Saddam! Saddam!"* and put his thumb down. *"No good!"*

The Bunkers

When the news broke that Saddam's soldiers were capitulating all across the Gulf War front—that they were not up for the fight, but were fleeing their bunkers, abandoning their equipment and surrendering themselves en masse—many armchair generals in the U.S.

In just about every bunker we cleared, there were a bunch of pictures of Madonna. I was like, "Wow!"

were quick to conjure up "What if..." scenarios, all basically asking, "What if the Iraqis had fought back?" But as our troops poured through shattered Iraqi defenses, they realized it could only have gone the way it had.

Throughout the war zone, most marines and soldiers gave a lot of credit to the Air War, which had literally annihilated the Iraqis' will to resist. But the efforts of the ground forces also earned *them* a good measure of recognition. For it was the shock of their lightning advance and the "now you see it, now you don't" wizardry of their high-tech weapons that actually brought most Iraqis scurrying out of their holes and into captivity.

If the doubting armchair generals had seen what our troops saw, they, too, would've understood the certainty in the unrelenting Desert Storm. One marine jumped into a bunker and found, prominently tacked to its southern wall, a full-page advertisement from an American magazine extolling the virtues of the Abrams M1-A1. He could only guess at how long the former occupants had stared the ad, before the frightening reality pulled up outside their back door.

In another bunker, a fellow marine discovered several cluster bomblets neatly lined up on the ledge of one of the shooting holes. And in the middle of the bunker's sand floor, he noticed an unexploded tank shell. It was half-buried in the sand, head-first, and all around it was a well-beaten path where the Iraqis had tread trying to avoid it. This marine could only guess that the shell was a dud which had, miraculously, come in through an open door or aperture. This bunker served as a real testimony to the joint war efforts of our air and ground forces.

As our troops combed the little Iraqi forts, they also came across some pretty outrageous stuff, the kinds of things they never would've expected in a million Muslim years.

Sgt. Ernie Grafton, combat photojournalist with the 2 MARDIV, turned up a pile of women's clothing, including a bra still in its box. "He must've been the camp pump," Ernie theorized.

In a nearby bunker, another marine turned up perfume and nightgowns. "That's where I got my XXX VCR tapes," he said.

Corporal Roush and his buddies from the 8th Tanks didn't find any female accoutrements, but they did turn up quite a collection of photos of a rock and roll queen.

"In just about every bunker we cleared," said Roush, "there were a bunch of pictures of Madonna. It looked like they were worshipping her. I was like, '*Wow!*' They had some *good* pictures!"

But not all the bunkers were so uptown. Many featured simpler displays, often pictures clipped from the lingerie sections of Sears and Monkey Ward catalogues.

All this pseudo-pornography left our troops pretty bewildered, after all they'd been hearing about Arab disdain for anything "suggestive."

However, one bunker must have housed some considerably more

*One marine found, tacked to the bunker wall,
a full-page advertisement from an American
magazine extolling the virtues of the M1-A1.*

orthodox guys. All it contained were Islamic-sanctioned female ankle shots—a whole bunker of just ankles?

One complex of bunkers had pictures of bare men plastered on their walls. "They were fascinated by muscle magazines," one soldier explained. "You'd go into a bunker, and they'd have wrestling and bodybuilding magazines. Almost invariably, every hole I went into, they had pictures of *guys.*"

Army Sgt. Kenneth Lowry told me of one other curiosity, which gave ample proof of the speed and terror of the coalition attack. Said Lowry, "We came in so fast that morning, some of the guys went into a bunker and found a toothbrush with toothpaste still on it!

"Somebody had been gettin' ready to brush his teeth, and then he hauled ass!"

The Spin

My wife saw and taped it. She said it was fan-fuckin'-tastic! And all it did was brag on the Marines!

> Gunny Cornwell, 8th Tanks
> on Stormin' Norman's
> Victory News Briefing

The Mother of All Bunkers

"It would be a shame to come this far and not step on the same tile as General Schwarzkopf," Army Maj. Mac Balod said, as we headed deep into the bowels of the MODA building, an acronym for the Saudi Ministry Of Defense and Aviation. This was also CENTCOM headquarters, and the underground bunker where the CINC hung his frequently televised hat. It was from here that the war had really been fought.

I was on my way down to the Graphics Department to visit with Tech Sgt. Tom "Zorro" Rominger, a friend I'd made during an earlier stay in Riyadh. Mac Balod handed me off to Tom at a sentry checkpoint, then Tom led me the rest of the way to his workshop.

"We're in a room that was used by the Saudi Arabians as a storage area," said Tom. "Fitting for a graphics shop. The lighting is pretty poor, but—hey, what the heck! We don't need good vision, do we? And we mopped it about a month ago. It's a shambles, but we're gettin' out of here so what does it matter?"

Then Tom introduced me to Army Sgt. Steve Alliman, who pointed to the "RESTROOM" sign on their door, and said, "It wasn't really the toilet. But we put the sign there, because this is where all the shit stops!"

Tom and Steve did all the graphics for General Schwarzkopf. And he saw every piece of work they did. "We're dealing with the real world," Steve said. "When people get shot down, and they need to put up a search and rescue, there's a lot of work here that goes into it.

"They'll come in there with their hair on fire, and we have to create maps and plot things. And people do get spun up. They get spun up a lot."

"You smoke a cigarette," added Tom, "look at them and laugh at them a little bit, and try to put it in perspective for them. Like an analyst."

Tom tried to put it in perspective for me. "You say, 'What *is* the problem?' And you get them to identify what it is they need. It's like a process.

"For example, somebody will say 'I've got a 30-slide briefing that the CINC's got to give to the chairman by 0-dark-30!' And he doesn't really know what it is that he wants to say. All he knows is that he has to do this, and he's putting you on alert.

"The first thing we know from experience is: he's lying," Tom continued. "The briefing isn't really due for three days, but he wants to have it finished in time to look at it again, and make any changes that he knows are gonna have to be made. So you try to get the truth out of him.

"'All right, what's your real 'suspense day'? What's the actual number you *really* need?'

"Because sometimes they come in with, 'We need thirty slides by 0-dark-30!' when they really need 90 slides. But they get their foot in the door with a *reasonable* request, and then it multiplies.

"It *always* multiplies, doesn't matter what it is. And you always know that once they do that, you're gonna work the night for them. You become their personal slave.

"Steve and I create 'final-product drafts' for them. They're not rough drafts, they're final products that they *use* as drafts. I wish we had an investment in the plastic companies that produced 35mm viewgraph slides. We'd be millionaires!"

The Mother of All Spins

Steve explained how they were constantly being asked to play "What If...?"

"We prepare a briefing on, say, what we're gonna do with the EPWs. We prepare an entire briefing in a Pro format, and an entire briefing in a Negative format, just in case the CINC wants to go either way. No one asks him which way he wants to go!"

"Oh, no! God forbid!" said Tom. "They say, 'We've got two plans for you, sir: plan #A and plan #B. You choose.'

"'Why didn't you ask me? You could've eliminated one of those plans.'

"'Oh, god! We didn't even think of that!'

201

"It's just like if the CINC needed a new car, and he said he liked Chevy's, they'd buy one of every Chevy, put them in the parking lot, and whichever one he walked up and got into, that was his. Oh, the rest of them? Well that's 'military spending,' what can we say?"

Then Steve remembered a little speech they'd been given one time, called "The Spin Factor."

"The CINC lobs the ball to the Chief of Staff," he said, "and gives it a couple of days. The Chief of Staff takes it, figures out which director it goes to, and says, 'Operations, we need you to work up a paper on this.'

"And he puts a little spin on the ball, so it picks up speed to *one* day.

"So the Chief of Operations, who sees everything that we do, goes, 'Okay, Current Ops? This is the plan, all right? This is what I think he wants.'

"And now it's down to a half a day. The full bird colonel director sends the ball to the action officer with a little more spin, and the ball's spinning even faster. So he's got a *few hours* to come up with the 'What if...?' plans for the CINC, and sends it to the graphics illustrator. When the ball finally comes to *us*, it's red hot!

"A hot project. You gotta get it done in *two hours*, so you bust your ass. You send it back with your mittens hot!

"It goes back to the action officer. He says, 'Oh, not quite,' and reverses the spin back to you.

"So you knock it out the way he wants it and send it to back to him.

"It goes back up and stops at the director: 'No, I don't quite think this is what the CINC wants.'

"He puts an overspin on the ball and sends it back. It comes back down at *MACH 4*.

"It goes all the way back up the chain of command in *one day*. It *should* have taken two. The Chief of Staff catches it, and just tosses it to the CINC, who goes, 'This is not what I asked for!'

"'The Mother of All Briefings' was the only time that didn't happen."

The Mother of All Briefings

Everybody in the world probably saw at least a few minutes of the "Mother of All Briefings" on TV, with all its charts and graphics. Well, it took five people and forty-eight hours, non-stop, to build it. Steve put in thirty-six hours himself.

"You know what our saving grace was on those charts we

We were all dog-tired of staring at those damn charts, but the CINC, like the chessmaster, was going over the plan he used to whup his opponent.

did?" asked Tom. "Rubber cement thinner. If we didn't have rubber cement thinner—and we'd didn't have much—we would *never* have been able to complete that job!"

"You'd have five units in a region," said Steve, "that have been there all along. They haven't changed or disappeared, they've always been there.

"But when you get to work, they tell you there's only four units there, and you put them down. Well, all of a sudden, two seconds before you're fixin' to go final, they ask you, 'Where's the fifth unit?'

"'You didn't *give* us a fifth unit! You gave us *four* units!'

"'Well, there's *always* been five units!'

"Suddenly, this fifth unit comes in and we're supposed to know about it! So it's a really good gift if you can read their minds—it's our hare-krishna thing: '*Hare-krishna! Hare-rama! Hold on! We're just picking up your thoughts! Oh, yeah.... Okay, I got it now.*'

"This was one of the rare times we got to work directly with *him*, one-on-one. It was a real kick, because he called me and said, '*You're* in charge of the project. Here's a full bird colonel from Operations and here's a full bird colonel from Intelligence. *They* are going to get you the information that *you* need to put it together. If *they* don't give you what *you* want, you tell *me!*'"

"It was great," said Steve, "because he came directly into our office, sat down at our table, and said, 'Okay, let's go over them one by one!' He went over it, narrating. The chief of staff goes, 'Well, we'll write you up a narration.'

"He goes, '*No, I don't need a narration. It's right here. Put it exactly the way I want it!*'

"So we put the things where he wanted them. Some major would come in and say, 'Hey, I don't think that's right.'

"We tell him, '*Piss off!* If the CINC wants it there, it's gonna stay there! *You* don't have four stars! I don't give a shit *what* you think! *This* is what the man wants and *this* is what he's gonna get! Period!'

"And the CINC was ecstatic with what he got," said Steve.

"At least we think he was," grinned Tom. "We didn't get fired or sent to KKMC!"

The Mother of All Burnouts

"Forty-seven and some-odd-hours later," Tom continued, "we were all dog-tired of looking at those charts. We couldn't *stand* them! But the CINC was in our office, talking about the damn war to us as he was describing what actually happened on those charts.

"He was like the chessmaster, going over the plan that he used to whup his opponent. But we didn't really give a rat's ass, because we'd been staring at those damn charts for the last two days! Our eyes were being held open with toothpicks, yet he's such a dynamic personality, you can't help but watch and listen.

"But in the back of your mind you're thinking, *Oh, come on! Just tell us it's okay and let us out of here! We want to go to sleep!*"

Then Steve explained the net result of his marathon effort. "After thirty-six hours straight of putting this briefing together for the CINC," he said, "I didn't even get to see it. I was asleep when he gave the briefing!"

A Fart in a Sandstorm

"You want to hear a Saddam joke?" asked the pretty Kuwaiti girl, Tania, as we sat with a bunch of Army guys in the shade of Kuwait City's burned-out International Hotel.

"Sure," I said, but I figured I'd already heard it. Seemed to me I'd heard every conceivable joke on Saddam by then. Our troops were full of them—though most of theirs were pretty raunchy and, often, bestiality-oriented.

"Okay," she said. "Saddam is in his bunker by himself, when Tariq Aziz rushes in the door. Aziz has one arm raised above his head with two fingers in the victory sign.

"Saddam looks up and says, 'We won?'

"'No,' says Aziz, 'there's just *two* of us left.'"

We all laughed. With the war just over, and Saddam's forces nearly obliterated, this seemed very funny. And I *hadn't* heard it before.

The more I talked with Tania, the more I understood what the Kuwaiti people had endured under Iraqi occupation. But "endured" is the wrong word. The Kuwaitis didn't just endure. They prevailed. Thanks in no small part to their irrepressible humor—like that I found in Tania's tales of certain bizarre incidents stemming from Saddam's invasion.

She told us of the morning the "butcher of Bagdad's" henchmen roared into Kuwait. She'd promised herself she would not work that day. She had a cold and needed the day off. But with the dawn came the first phone call.

"The Iraqis are in Kuwait!" her sister screamed.

"Oh, sure," Tania mumbled. Then she hung up, pulled the phone cord from the wall and went back to sleep.

Two hours passed before the maid came into her room shouting that her sister had called back on the other phone. The Iraqis were now all over Kuwait City, some even in Tania's neighborhood. She crawled out of bed, dressed, and started downtown.

As Tania walked through the city, she saw Iraqi soldiers with machine guns everywhere—and lots of tanks, armored personnel carriers, helicopters and jet aircraft. An old Kuwaiti man came running down the boulevard toward her, waving his Arab head scarf and hollering, *"Iraqis in Kuwait! Iraqis in Kuwait!"*

Days later, after Saddam had all of Kuwait firmly in his grasp, he began replacing the Republican Guards who had led the invasion with troops of a lower caliber. Most of these replacements were peasants from rural Iraq. They had little education and even less experience in urban environments. Much of the Kuwaiti humor

With Saddam's forces nearly obliterated, the Kuwaiti girl's joke seemed very funny.

during the occupation was generated by these peasant soldiers as they bumbled around in a thoroughly modern Kuwait City.

Tania remembered passing by one of her country's leading banks and overhearing one Iraqi soldier say to another by the automatic bank teller, "Holy shit, Ahkmed! See how rich those Kuwaitis are? Even their walls spit money!"

One of Tania's friends passed the same spot sometime later and observed another Iraqi with a cup jammed into the same auto-teller, waiting for it to dispense a shot of hot coffee.

Another time, Tania was in a small grocery store where a couple of soldiers were demanding that the clerk give them all the canned tuna fish he had stacked behind the counter: "Those ones," the Iraqis yelled, "the tuna cans with the little cats on them!"

Then there was the Kuwaiti guy Tania knew who, before leaving home one morning, stowed a case of dog food under his kitchen table. When he returned he found empty dog food cans scattered all over the place—and the toilet clogged with vomit.

But the Iraqis' favorite snack was what they believed to be white cream cheese in plastic tubes. It turned out to be Nivea skin cream, and many of the Iraqis ended up in Kuwait City hospitals, getting their stomachs pumped.

While these displays of ignorance took their toll on the Iraqi occupation forces, they were merely—as one 2 MARDIV corporal put it—"a fart in a sandstorm compared to the real shit that happened later."

He was referring to when the Iraqis tried to *unoccupy* Kuwait via the infamous "Highway to Hell."

It's News to Us!

My first contact with the press in country came shortly after I arrived. Glenn and I were asked to join a mostly Saudi contingent of journalists who were flying into Kuwait, courtesy of the Royal Saudi Air Force, to survey the devastation along the "Highway to Hell." The war had been over for nearly two weeks, but just the day before the last corpses had been removed from the scene.

As we dismounted from our tour bus and began threading our way through the area, we were absolutely stunned by the extent of the destruction. Wherever we looked there were crumpled, shredded, pock-marked vehicles. What once had been trucks, tanks, armored personnel carriers, school busses, pick-ups, and sedans, now were just shattered hulks, strewn about grotesquely. And, on all sides, littering the roadway, were remnants of the plunder the Iraqis had tried to take back home. I saw baby toys, engine starters, TVs, VCRs, sacks of potatoes, civilian clothes, notebooks, tires—anything and everything you could imagine.

Apparently, Saddam's soldiers had just begun fleeing Kuwait City when they were spotted by our aircraft. Throughout that night and the next day they were pummeled from above by all of our military branches, using whatever ordnance was available. The first bombs struck the head of the column, halting the looters' progress. Then, the enemy soldiers behind were caught in a terrifying gridlock—sitting ducks is what they were. Hence, the flyers' name for the Iraqi disaster, "The Traffic Jam."

Meanwhile, on the ground, the 1 MEF Marines and the Army's Tiger Brigade flailed away at the enemy with artillery, tanks, and every other bit of firepower they could bring to bear. When it was all over, these troops were among the first to view the site of the slaughter up close. Looking over the carnage around them, they dubbed the place, "Clusterfuck Junction."

As we continued our tour of the scene, we noticed unexploded ordnance everywhere, mostly from cluster bombs. Mixed in with the little bomblets were all sorts of hand grenades and RPGs, which the Iraqis never had time to use.

The Saudi press was particularly fascinated by the grenades. One of their reporters hauled a whole box of them out of the back of an Iraqi APC, then playfully began tossing them to his friends for souvenirs. The Royal Air Force crew that later flew us back to Riyadh must have been savvy to what was going on, because they frisked each and every one of us before we climbed back aboard.

Eventually, almost all of the media in theater had a chance to visit the Highway to Hell. And many of them, like the Saudis, tried to collect a few souvenirs in the process—which is probably why the following joke began to circulate among the troops: "I hear Saddam Hussein used to have the fourth largest army in the world, but now CBS does." There were a *lot* of "fourth largest army" jokes floating around at the time.

For the most part, our troops had few nice things to say about the press. I'm not just talking about the Public Affairs troops, whose job was to contend with the endless stream of reporters—many of whom showed up in the field poorly equipped in their knowledge of military operations, but locked and loaded with inane questions.

No, I'm talking here about your average troop, who was genuinely frightened of what lay ahead, but still was willing to put his life on the line, because that was his job. Yet every time he got a glimpse of the news, over a ready room TV, or in a dog-eared paper, or through a letter from home, he was confronted with people better informed on the war than he was himself. Most troops would've shared the consternation of the young lieutenant who felt *he* should have heard from his superiors about the war starting up, before he heard it on the news.

Sgt. Kevin Green of the Tiger Brigade was similarly frustrated by the information gap, and had been since he first deployed on October 5th. "As soon as we got here," he told me, "everything was a secret! It was, 'Don't write home this. Don't write home that. Don't write home how we're going to be attached to the Marines.' But every time I got a letter from my wife, she was telling what I didn't even know yet!"

Sgt. Scott A. Smith, of the 4th Marine TOWs, was particularly upset with the way the press badgered the military briefers:

> I was listening to the news briefing after the war, and they were talking about all the different guidelines that they were setting up for the peace proposal.
>
> And everybody kept needling the briefer, asking "What if *this* happens?"
>
> He kept saying, "Well, you can't build this on 'what ifs'! This is what we've set down. When 'what if' comes up, then we'll take actions toward it."
>
> Then the next person asked basically the same thing. And I was like, "Man! Why don't those guys just *quit?* If he starts telling where everybody's at and exactly what they're doing, he's endangering their *lives!*"

*Many reporters showed up in the field poorly
equipped in their knowledge of military operations.*

The press just wouldn't let him alone. Finally he just
said, "I'm done answering your questions," and walked off.
The press just had no respect for the secrecy of things.

According to Smith, in the Gulf, CNN stood for "Classified News
Network."

But it wasn't only classified information, which the press had and
the troops lacked, that riled the servicemen.

"I tell you what," said Sergeant Smith, "I wished I was a news
personnel. Right before the war started, I was lookin' at all the gear
we were missing, and the press seemed to have it on!"

One big bone of contention with the marines concerned a piece
of gear called the "ninja" jacket, a new field coat designed to improve
a troop's chances of avoiding detection in the dark. Supposedly,
these jackets were in short supply, though members of the media
seemed to have them.   SSgt. Larry Neel, also of the 4th TOWs,

remembered a time when the press got the scoop on this matter, loud and clear:

> There was a CNN girl who had on one of those green parkas the marines wear. She was all serious but couldn't get people to interview, because the lieutenant had just briefed them about heading up north. Finally she got the movie camera on one guy and asked him what he thought about the latest peace proposal.
>
> And all he could say was, "Where'd you get that jacket you're wearing!"
>
> And she said, "Well, it got issued to me—"
>
> *"Oh, it DID, huh?"* he drilled her. *"They just ISSUED that jacket to ya?"*
>
> She was trying to get an interview out of him, but he just started raising hell with her.

Neel also explained that, at that time, the marines had just five days before "we were goin' in after 'em, no matter what."

"But," he said, "the CNN guys were askin' us questions like, 'What do you think of the latest peace offer?'

"I smiled at 'em and said, 'Hell, *it* don't matter!'"

Even when a troop was anxious to be interviewed, the news person involved often got more than she or he bargained for. Take the marine that Maj. Roger "Hump Monster" Humphreys, of the HML-767, watched on the squadron TV:

> After they had the Khafji battle, some female TV reporter was interviewing a young Marine corporal, who was manning a TOW on the highway to Kuwait City. She said, "They've come across the border now, and you beat them back. What are you gonna do if they come across again?"
>
> He looked up the highway, and said, "Well, if a bad guy comes down that road, and I know he's a bad guy, and I have permission to shoot, *I'm gonna take that bad boy out*—that's *exactly* what's gonna happen."
>
> She swallowed nervously and went, "Uhhhh...back to you, Peter!"

Our British allies also had their problems with the media. But, with typical Brit resignation and wit, Signalman Neil Caddy of the 1st UK Armored Division showed me he was always ready to cooperate:

> They're a necessary evil, and it's up to us to ensure that they get the best chance to do their job.
>
> Yet, they always get in the bloody way, don't they?

However well you arrange the thing, whatever press facility you lay on, they will *always* be in the way. They will always be a boil on the bum!

Still, the press didn't just give the troops headaches, they also gave them a lot of laughs. Capt. Ed Kujat of the USS *Foster* remembered such an occasion when he and a few of his officers watched a taped re-run of a CNN report:

Right after a SCUD attack, there was a CNN reporter doing a live, stand-up interview from Riyadh. In the middle of the interview, he thought he smelled something funny and felt kind of dizzy.

While the guy being interviewed was standing there talking to the people back in Washington, the reporter suddenly dropped to his knees and pulled out his gas mask and slapped it on. This was in front of live television! For those of us who weren't watching it live, it looked somewhat humorous, but I'm sure for him it wasn't humorous at the time.

I think the person who was even more shocked was the guy that was standing next to him. He just kept on talking to Washington!

The captain's story reminded me of something Glenn Eure had told me earlier. He said you could always tell the new media from the old in the Gulf by their first reactions to a SCUD attack. "When an alert sounded," said Glenn, "the new guys grabbed for their gas masks, while the old guys grabbed for their helmets."

The troops also got a laugh from the way the media would fumble the facts: like the New Orleans reporter who wrote in his paper that the A-10 was a Mach 3 fighter. Out at King Fahd, the guys who flew the Warthogs loved it.

"A Mach 3 fighter? Yeah. Uh-huh. Sure!" grinned Lt. Mike Larkin of the 706th Cajuns. "But they printed it!"

The pilots knew all too well that, even in the longest, steepest of dives, the plane couldn't dream of hitting Mach 1, never mind *three* times the speed of sound. In fact, much of the Warthog's "reputation" rested on it being the slowest fighter in our Gulf inventory.

"They just had so little idea of what they were talking about!" added Larkin. Then he told me another media tale about the A-10. This one was a TV blooper:

The NBC morning news was talking about the A-10s from some undisclosed Middle East base, and you could see the planes in the background.

Bryant Gumble turned to the female reporter and asked her, "Well, do they have any particular problems there?"

There was a momentary pause for the time lapse, and, suddenly, she comes on and says, "Yes, as a matter of fact, Bryant, the maintenance people are having a lot of difficulty with the sand and the heat, and the problems they're causing for the A-10's radar system."

We all sat there for a moment and looked at each other. *A-10s don't have radar. A-10s will never have radar!*

Captain Kujat remembered one reporter who remarked that the United States was floating every ship it could muster, "even old minesweepers with wooden hulls." Kujat had to chuckle, because boats used for picking up and clearing mines are purposely built with wooden hulls, so they won't attract and explode the things.

I'm sure many of the news people themselves joked about the inaccuracies. By and large, I found those press guys to be a pretty humorous bunch of characters—that is, when they weren't trying to claw their way into some kind of interview or camera angle.

Out at Al Kharj Air Base, I saw a sign one of them had mounted on his press vehicle. It read:

IF IT'S NEWS, IT'S NEWS TO US!

The Shaft

We came, we won, we waited...

Lt. Col. Kas Jasczczak
Wing Commander, Al Kharj Air Base

Sick Call

Everyone says when they leave they don't ever want to see sand again. But someday they'll look back at what happened here, and they'll be proud to say—"We did it, and we did it in the sand."

Capt. L. R. Leslie,
CO, Fleet Hospital 15

Once the ceasefire was in effect, our military leaders began totaling up their gains and losses. By the time Glenn and I arrived at Fleet Hospital 15 in mid-March, the medical staff had already reached a bottom line for the war. Navy Lt. Charles Knight, part of the emergency room crew, gave me a summary.

"Total patients through this ER were around 3,500," he said. "We saw eighty percent of all the Marine casualties taken in-theater during the war, and didn't lose *any* of them. We did lose one Saudi."

"Not a bad batting average, Lieutenant," chuckled Glenn, "unless you were the Saudi."

Later, while eating lunch in the local chow hall, I visited with WO Bill Racy, a Seabee assigned to the hospital's "Public Works" department. Racy explained the reaction of most marines when they first encountered this very civilized environment.

> The first thing they'd like to do was hit our showers, 'cause we had good shower facilities.
>
> Then they got in the chow line as many as three times, and ate a good, hot meal. They just couldn't get enough of the good, home-cooked food.
>
> And somewhere in that hierarchy of needs, one of the things they wanted to do was look at all the nurses and savor their appearance.

Nurses were always a high priority on any male troop's sick call itinerary anywhere. Often these were the first females, who looked and smelled and spoke like females, that the frontline marines and soldiers had seen in months.

Depending on the nature of his ailment, often the troop's own buddies found it necessary to haul him in for medical care themselves.

The dentist immediately dropped everything
and found out what I needed.

And lucky was the troop who had his friends there with him to cheer him up—and share his view of those nurses.

Except, maybe, when his unit was the HML-767, which could never resist leaving its own zany impression on a hospital visit—make that, on a hospital night stand. Maj. Charlie "Tuna Man" Ward told me of a set of such impressions:

> When we were moving down from Lonesome Dove back to Al Jubail, repositioning after the Ground War was over, one of the guys slipped a disk in his back. So we loaded him on one of the birds and took him down to the hospital, and they stuck him in there for almost a week and a half. He was getting all the female nurses' attention.
>
> We had a couple of rubbers that Jimbo had gotten in the mail. The guy couldn't move in his bed, so we set those rubbers right there on his night stand, where he couldn't see them, but the nurses couldn't miss them!

Evidently, a nurse came in that night, saw them there, and moved them back a little bit out of the way. Of course he would get up at certain times during the day, and they'd make him walk for five or ten minutes, and then they'd kick him flat on his back.

We went over to visit him the next night, but he'd seen the rubbers and took 'em off. So we put some more out!

And when he came back to the unit a week and a half later, he was hot! *"Okay, you sons of bitches,"* he said, *"who the fuck put those rubbers out?"*

But evidently the nurses loved it!

Sergeant Malloy, of the 595th Medical Company (Clearing), told me of the time he dropped in on a frontline hospital that treated EPWs as well as our guys. Though Malloy wasn't in for health care, he was in for an education:

When we pulled into 5th MASH, they were taking enemy POWs. There were a couple of American casualties, but not many. The soldiers, eager as they were, would go and volunteer to help the 5th MASH—or, to help the nurses—to get medical training, which I guess was a good idea.

I walked in, and there was one Iraqi, who didn't look too bad. He had a couple of little shrapnel burns on his face. And there was a female soldier, probably a nurse, very well endowed on the top, and she was bending down to fix his IV.

So there was this Iraqi with this big smile on his face, as he was being buried by her jugs, and I was thinkin' to myself, *You slimeball! I've been in country for five months now, and you've got more than me—and you're the enemy!*

Sometimes it wasn't just an IV that a patient would receive from a nurse, or just a look that he would give her. Pappy Husty of HMA-775 recalled a time when a SCUD alert sounded in the area, and an airman and a nurse were trapped together in a foxhole:

When the SCUD alarm went off, and they were over there with each other, they jumped down in a hole. He stayed in the hole with her. And next thing you knew, both of their masks were off and so were their pants, and they were going at it. It was good for morale, but...

But the sick call of all sick calls that I encountered in the Gulf didn't involve a single nurse. Nor, as Groucho Marx might've said, a married one.

No, the "Mother of All Sick Calls" involved a dentist. And never in the annals of war had a sick call patient ever travelled so far, so forward, and for so little in the way of results, than did Sgt. Jerry McCrudden, when he tried to find himself a little dental care. McCrudden smiled as he elaborated on it:

> I needed to get some bridgework done, but back here in Dharan they couldn't treat me. So I got sent up to King Khalid Military City, to see a particular dentist.
>
> Well, that particular dentist had moved from KKMC to Log Base Charlie (a forward supply depot—*very* forward). So I went out and caught a medevac helicopter up to Log Base Charlie. The helicopter was on a medevac mission, and, after he dropped me off, the pilot had to go ten miles west of Log Base Charlie to pick up two patients. But he said he'd pick me up on the way back—if he could—and transport me back to KKMC.
>
> Well, on the way up to Log Base Charlie, I'd said to the pilot, "Well, just to expedite my chances of getting a ride back, let's call ahead and see if the dentist is available to treat me."
>
> I don't know if the pilot heard me and called it in, but when I got off the helicopter and went into the treatment facility, the dentist immediately dropped everything, put me in the chair, found out what I needed. Then, the first comment out of his mouth was, *"Who's the fucking idiot who sent you up here?"*
>
> I explained to him what the Doc had sent me up there for, but he told me, "There's not a damn thing I can do for you at the front that couldn't be done back there!"

Among My Souvenirs

I don't want to bring people home in body bags because of their stupidity. The war is over. Let's get the hell out of here.

SSgt. Scott Beauchemin
8th Tank Bn., 2 MARDIV

The only discouraging words I heard concerning General Schwarz-kopf as I roamed the Arabian Peninsula were spoken by some of the same marines he had spoken of earlier with pride. They were complaining about the CENTCOM directive prohibiting certain souvenirs, particularly sand. Said one 8th Tanker:

They tell us that we can't even take the damn sand as a souvenir for our relatives—that some people out here *died* for liberating this country. What burned my ass was when General Schwarzkopf got down on his knees and filled up a little beaker of sand to take home!

"That's Rule Number One," added another marine, referring to the list of rules Central Command had circulated around the theater, distinguishing contraband from legal souvenirs. I was shown a copy of that list, and there it was, right at the top of the column of forbidden items—"NO Sand."

However, there was a consensus of opinion among these marines that it wasn't the general's idea for him to have sand while they couldn't. "I think it's the ones underneath him," one grunt muttered.

Sand was only one of the outlawed items that the troops found unfair. Most soldiers also wanted to head home with an AK-47, or at least with the bayonet off one. But both of these items were also listed as forbidden. Again injustice seemed to raise its ugly head.

"We can't have any of these weapons welded up as souvenirs," one soldier explained, "and yet they took, as trophies, one of every weapon we captured to the Secret Service that was guarding the ambassador. They just loaded them up in the back of a truck and took off with them."

One item on the list that I found pretty strange was "NO Treasonable Literature." What the hell it meant, no one seemed to know. But it was listed all the same, third from the top, right above "NO Force Labor Literature"—whatever the hell *that* was.

220

However, in spite of the CENTCOM mandate against contraband weapons, a lot of troops tried to *sneak* them home. Though, usually, they'd only make it as far as one of the redeployment compounds, like Khobar Towers. Hardly the best place to have second thoughts and casually discard things that went "Bang!"

One evening, while out strolling around the Khobar compound, I passed a sentry bunker and overheard some radio traffic concerning a hand grenade discovered in a dumpster:

> *"Where is it now? Is it still in the mound, or have you actually moved it? Over."*
>
> *"We used a stick to move away the debris that was on top of it, and the grenade itself rolled over a little bit. I'm looking at it right now, I'm sittin' right above it. The spoon itself is inside the grenade, and the rest of it is on the outside of it. It's not activated at all. There's no fuse inside of it."*
>
> *"Okay, be advised that those fuses are unstable. If there's a fuse anywhere around there, don't touch it. Over."*

It seems that one of the more popular last-minute options for disposing of forbidden souvenirs was to toss them into the trash. As you can gather from the transmission above, this wasn't considered a safe alternative. Sgt. Michael Bitando of the 800th MPs showed me pictures of some throwaways he had turned up.

"These are AK-47s and 7.62 RPG rounds," Bitando explained. "I found them in the dipsy dumpsters. We have sixty-eight weapons now confiscated from dumpsters—all stuff the troops were trying to take back to the states."

But it wasn't just small arms the troops were trying to take home. Just as Radar O'Reilly in *M*A*S*H* tried to ship home a jeep from Korea, many troops in the Gulf also tried for bigger souvenirs, or "trophies." Usually it was done as a unit project and with appropriate authorization—*usually.*

One case where the authorization was doubtful involved a doctor from the 511th Tactical Fighter Squadron at King Fahd, Major William Alden Smith. The Doc assumed he had the right to secure a trophy for his squadron. And what would be the most fitting trophy for the A-10 guys who had swarmed over the Iraqi AAA like a flock of vultures? Doc told me all about it:

> Randy Dickman and I flew into Kuwait City, and were talking with one of the Explosive Ordnance Disposal members. He asked us, "Would you like to have a trophy for your squadron?"

"Sure," I said. "Let me clear it with my squadron." So I called for permission to get a trophy.

Well, it turned out to be a four-gun ZPU—a 14.5 mm, 2–ton, towed antiaircraft gun.

By hook and crook and some bribery, I got an Army Chinook helicopter company to graciously fly it down here. But when the wing duty officer heard about it, he hit the ceiling. They restricted me to base *by name*.

I think I'm the only flight surgeon in theater who was restricted to base.

According to Dickman, one of Doc Smith's medical colleagues, it raised a lot of hell with the troops when Doc was restricted to base over the trophy.

"You know how they got signs on the gates saying, 'NOT ONE MORE LIFE'?" Dickman asked me, referring to the military's campaign slogan aimed at eliminating accidental post-war casualties. "Well, we were gonna make up signs that said, 'NOT ONE MORE DOCTOR!' and 'FREE DOC SMITH!'"

Apparently signals were crossed between the different Air Force bases, because down at Al Kharj a similar trophy was requisitioned, with little flak for anyone involved. Capt. Ray Smith, of the 335th TFS Chiefs, gave me the story behind their find:

A friend of ours happened to be working with the Army guys right outside of Kuwait City when they took over. Later, when he was down here visiting us, he said, "Come on! I'll take you up there, and we'll get some souvenirs!"

The CO said, "Okay, I'll let you go if you guys can bring back an AAA gun."

So, at four in the morning, five of us piled into a jeep and headed up to Kuwait. After a long and exhausting trip, we got there and started digging around in bunkers.

Finally, we came across the AAA piece you see sittin' out here. It took us two hours to dig the gun out. There was live ammunition *everywhere* so we checked it to make sure it was unloaded. We hooked it up to the back of the jeep, and went flying out of there.

On the way out, we were trying to get over these little ditches, and the guy who was drivin' was just a maniac. We were airborne, the AAA piece was airborne, and the guys in the jeep behind us swore we were gonna die, because the AAA kept comin' up and almost hittin' the top of the jeep!

Though collecting souvenirs could indeed be hazardous, there was a far greater danger for those in command to control—namely, carelessness. In the face of a long, uncertain wait to get home, people

222

We have sixty-eight weapons confiscated—all stuff the troops were trying to take back to the states.

were often very careless, trying reckless things they'd never thought of doing in combat. And some of them died in the process.

While at Khobar, PFC Brian Bess told me what had happened to some soldiers who were thoughtlessly horsing around with mines:

> One of them picked up the mine by the ribbon and started swinging it around. It blew his head off and wounded his buddy.
>
> There was another guy who picked a mine up, and was flipping it up in his hands. It blew his hands off, and the shrapnel hit him in the stomach.

Later, over in Riyadh, I touched on the same topic with CENTCOM artists Steve Alliman and Tom Rominger. Even after the war ended, these guys were doing regular morning casualty reports for the CINC, because people were still being injured and killed in accidents.

"General Schwarzkopf gets really ticked every time he sees an accidental death," said Steve.

"He takes it as a personal loss," Tom added. "And they've had some really stupid fatalities, things that should've been avoided."

In one such "stupid fatality," an MP lieutenant was showing off the safety features of the .45 pistol he carried. He placed the barrel of the gun up to an object to illustrate how the .45 wouldn't fire with its nose pressed tightly against something. He squeezed the trigger, but the hammer wouldn't fall. It worked. Next he pressed the barrel up to his head and pulled the trigger.

"He blew his brains out," said Steve. "It was a senseless loss of life. General Schwarzkopf said at one of the briefings right after the war, *'Look! Take the damn weapons away from them! If you people can't control them, you're gonna start answering to me!'*

"I mean, he was ready to fire *commanders*," recalled Steve. "A lot of people think it's for show when he says that on TV. But in the war room, as I flipped the slides for him, sitting on a stool not three feet away, I've seen his eyes fill up with tears. He got really angry, because the commanders were not doing their job and protecting their troops."

When I get home...

Thoughts of returning home filled the minds of our troops well before they ever set foot in Saudi Arabia or sailed into the Persian Gulf.

The sheer numbers in their deployment had spoken eloquently to them. This wasn't to be another simple "overnighter," like Grenada or Panama. And ominous comparisons to the interminable Vietnam experience were all too easily conjured up.

Then the official word came down: "The only way home is through Iraq!" And the troops buckled down for the long haul ahead.

But the Ground War was over in 100 hours! At first nobody could believe it, neither the generals nor the grunts. Then, as the ceasefire settled in over the peninsula, the focus shifted dramatically from getting Saddam to getting home.

The worst part now for the troops, as they waited to get their return-trip tickets punched, was not knowing *when* it would happen. Two days? Two months? Christmas? It was particularly hard on the reservists, who had left not only their families behind but regular jobs and businesses as well.

There seemed to be no hard and fast rule for who would go when or why. At one point it was rumored that the "warriors go first." Yet warrior outfits like the Marine Reserve's 8th Tanks, who had been first to breach the Iraqi defenses, remained stalled in the sickly air of Kuwait for many weeks, while rear-echelon support units flew out regularly.

Even worse than waiting for the word was getting the wrong word. Sgt. Darin "Chico" Gallow of the "Powerline" at King Aziz got the word that he'd be stateside on a specific day in April—only to have the word change at the last minute, as his wife and kids were in mid-flight to California to greet him. "Another six weeks," the marine was told.

At this point, the Pentagon was labeling the final phase of the war "Desert Calm." But to Sergeant Gallow, the 8th Tanks, and tens of thousands of other frustrated troops, it was known as "Desert Shaft."

That was the reality of the situation. Now let me share a little of the fantasy with you, the stuff dreams were made of as the troops prepared for the big redeployment home:

Lt. John Butler, 595th Medical Company (Clearing):
I'm the only single guy of the four of us that ride around together all the time. Dr. Heidenberg is 32 goin' on 48, a

little older than he looks. He's been giving me a lot of sound advice on how to be a single man in the '90s.

We decided the best thing for me to do as a single guy, HIV negative, in this modern time was to go back to a good bar that I've been to before and, without bringing too much

The worst part now for the troops, as they waited to get their return-trip tickets punched, was not knowing when it would happen.

attention to myself, get up in front of the people and say, "Uh, look. I just spent six or seven months over in the desert for Desert Shield and Desert Storm. And, uh, I'm not looking for any sympathy or anything like that, but I would like the company of one young, brave female who's willing to put her money where her mouth is. You know, we've heard a lot of stories about yellow ribbons and American flags, and we've gotten a lot of "Any Soldier" mail, and it's time for someone to back that up. But I'm not looking for a relationship...."

GSM3 Howard E. Forepaugh, USS Foster:

The best thing about getting home is you won't have to watch TV with thirty other guys. You can change the channel to what you *want*. You can eat what you *want*, and not at the designated mealtimes. And if you *want*, you can have that late snack.

GS2 Leif Sabo, USS Foster:

When I get home the first thing I'll do is have *sex*. Then I'll put my bags down.

Capt. Douglas "Tonto" Dry, XO, 4th TOWs, 2 MARDIV:

I want to run for tribal chief. I was supposed to before, but then I got "drafted."

GSM1 Nathan Oman, USS Foster:

Just gettin' off the ship would be the first goal in my life, but I would seriously like to get out and do some hunting. I want to go kill something.

Sgt. Scott A. Smith, 4th TOWs, 2 MARDIV:

I can't wait to get home so I can look at tapes of CNN and read old newspapers to figure out just exactly what went on over here. I figure Time/Life books will have *The Four Day War* out before I get home.

Sgt. Michael Baldasarre, 4th Marines, 2 MARDIV:

Guys say, "Hey, yeah! When we get back we can join the VFW." And you think, "I was actually in a *war!*" Doesn't seem like it, really.

Corporal Angelone, 4th Marines, 2 MARDIV:

We made up a dance out here that we're gonna do when we all get back to Jacksonville. It's a combination of the "Camel Strut" and "Ski Poles at the Ready." You gotta have the right music.

SSgt. Jeffrey "Hey" Wire, 1st Bn., 67th Reg, Tiger Bde.:

When we get home, we're all gonna picket the MRE plant in San Antonio.

Lt. Col. Dick Cody, CO, 1st Bn., 101st Aviation Regiment:

When we go back to Ft. Campbell, we're gonna have a party down in Nashville...in a *parking garage down there!*

The Love Boat

At the outset of Desert Shield, it was apparent to the brass that the troops were in for a long, grueling deployment. Therefore, they quickly began a search for suitable diversions from the stresses inherent to such a prolonged ordeal. In the past, such diversions had always been cheerfully provided by the destination country. But not so this time.

Traditional troop diversions were strictly off limits in the Saudi Kingdom. There would be no weekend drunks or public consorting between the sexes as long as the soldiers, sailors, marines and airmen were on the Saudis' turf. So it was abundantly clear that *something* had to be found to compensate, or there'd be a lot of unhappy campers to control.

By war's end, a number of compensating diversions were operational in the Gulf. The best known of these was the "Love Boat." Thanks to the Cunard Line, and the American taxpayers, hundreds of troops from all over the theater were regularly piped aboard the *Princess* cruise ship, where they could eat, drink, and go nuts for three glorious days.

Now, let me take you aboard the Love Boat:

SSgt. Rick Torres, Powerline, VMA 311:
After seven and a half months being here, they sent us down to Bahrain, where the Cunard *Princess* was docked. They tried to send all the junior people.

I didn't want to go. I didn't argue with the sergeant-major, but I told him, "Sergeant-Major, I don't want to go!"

And he said, "You're going on liberty!"

"But, sir," I responded. "I don't want to go on liberty!"

Basically, we all just wanted to go home. We were just sitting here in limbo. They didn't want to send us home—they wanted to send us on the Love Boat!

It was like somebody said, "Goddamn it, there *will be morale!* We'll send these guys on the Love Boat!"

You walked up the ramp and the first thing they did was snap a picture of you. Then they shook your hand and said, "Welcome aboard! Can we help you?"

I was thinking, *Where's Captain Steubing at? This is great!* It was just like on TV.

Here I was, coming out of nowhere. I'd been walking around in a tent and dirt for seven and a half months. Now I was aboard a nice ship, around women who smelled good—not women marines, *real* women—and people who were clean. It was totally weird, like bein' in a time warp.

You had to buy your drinks, but the food was free. They even let you have clothes for free.

In those three nights, we tried to make up for seven and a half months of not drinking—if you could picture jarhead marines doing that! So, from sun up, we'd start drinking.

All we wanted to do was drink and see some women. But they had beer belly contests. And they put ping-pong balls in the pool, and guys would jump in and stuff as many ping-pong balls in their shorts as they could. The girls would say, "Oh my, you have big balls!"

They didn't have very many women there, so they did the best they could to keep all those Army, Navy, Air Force and Marine guys occupied. And you could see how stupid we were acting. Everybody was half drunk and stupid.

It was a nice getaway from the desert. It was almost a taste of home. It was definitely a welcome change, if you could imagine living in the desert for seven months.

But believe it or not, I was happy when it was over. I couldn't have lasted another three days or three nights!

Marine Capt. Shawn "Schotz" Wiedenhoeft, VMA 311:

I got picked because I was a junior pilot. The XO came into my hooch, and there were a bunch of other pilots sittin' around. He looked at me and goes, "Schotz, you want to go on the Love Boat?"

I started thinking about it, because I would have felt really guilty about going when everybody else had to stay in camp.

But, almost in unison, three other pilots went, *"Is this a trick question? Of course he wants to go!"* So I went.

I got married by proxy, through the mail. I'd been engaged a couple months before the Iraqis attacked Kuwait, and we'd been planning on getting married in November. So when I came out here, we'd decided to put it off. But after awhile, she wanted to get married and I wanted to get the money started.

She went up to Colorado, since it's legal there, and she got the paperwork done. I got it in the mail, filled it out, had it notarized, and sent it back, designating her uncle as my proxy.

So on December 29th, she and her uncle walked down the aisle. The first thing she said over the phone was, "I'm now deductible!" Got the money started and a break on my taxes. What else could you ask for? A honeymoon?

Well, a lot of guys were calling the Love Boat cruise my "honeymoon by proxy!"

TSgt. Tom "Zorro" Rominger, CENTCOM:
The day that I went down there was during the Passover holiday, so the first thing that happened before I boarded the boat was a Jewish rabbi asked me if I was Jewish. I thought that it was going to be strange situation—here I am in the middle of an Arab world, being asked by a rabbi if I'm Jewish or not.

I told him I wasn't, and he said, "Well, it's okay. You can tell us."

"No, really," I said. "I'm not!"

And it turned out that, of the nine hundred people on the boat, seven hundred of them were Jewish. So, you know, it was interesting. Like shopping in New York. It was wonderful! Yet they still had bacon for breakfast in the morning for us, so it wasn't a problem.

The first thing I noticed as I got on were all the women, working behind the desk. I was amazed. They had a PX and a finance office there—everything you'd need to make it a home for yourself for those three days.

Then I went straight to the bar, and had myself some drinks. The buffet was this huge line of food, about twenty-five meters' worth. You couldn't see the other end. There were just too many people, too much food, and plants and things in the way. So I grabbed a plate and started walkin' around, piling food on. When I got to the end, this guy grabbed my plate out of my hand.

I was like, "Hey, bud, what are you *doing?*"

He goes, "I'm gonna take you to your table."

I said, "That's okay, I don't even *have* a table yet."

He goes, "Well, I'm gonna pick one out for you."

I said, "I'm perfectly capable of finding a table for myself."

"No-no-no," he says. "That's my *job!*"

It *was* their job, you know. They wore jackets and bow ties, and they'd grab your plate and take you to your table. But nobody told us that, nobody warned us.

There was one marine who didn't appreciate it *at all* when the guy grabbed his plate. I thought there was gonna be a fight, especially after he'd had a few drinks at the bar!

Cpl. Jerona Roman, VMA 311:
Let me talk about this "Love Boat," man.

After bein' here for seven months, they just decide to

There was one marine who didn't appreciate
it at all when the guy grabbed his plate.

send me on the Love Boat and get me some R-n-R.
Everybody was lookin' forward to gettin' on the Love Boat,
'cause it didn't come to us every damn week.

The sergeant major said, "Yeah, Roman, you're gonna
get on the Love Boat, go to some port some place, they'll let
you off, and you're gonna have a real nice time!"

I said, "What? You gonna send me with some of my
friends?"

They said, "No."

I said, "Well, goddamn! I'll just make the best of the
situation." So I go on this "Love Boat."

Now they say you're gonna have three days and four
nights. It took us a whole day to get to the damn *boat!* I
said, "Three days an' four nights, and I just spent *today*
trying to get *to* this motha. That was one of my damn
days?"

Okay, finally we get on the damn ship. I go to my damn

room, case the joint, check it out real quick, and go get me something to eat. After that, I headed straight to the damn bar.

Now, this ship's got five bars. Nice bars. They got a comedy section, a bar up on the poolside, a disco, a bar that's indoor-outdoor—and I don't know what else they got, but they got two more, and every one of these mothafuckers is different. Some people had a good time, and some didn't. But I had a good time, because I drank my ass off. I owed it to myself.

Gettin back on the subject, there was this dude named "Marrow" from Ordnance. Ordnance people are always gettin' in trouble.

Two o'clock was when they closed the disco lounge. They gave you till two-thirty to get in your damn room. All right. I'm in my damn room, and suddenly I hear all this noise out in the hall. There was some master sergeant of the Air Force out there yellin', "GET IN YOUR ROOM! HEY! GET— GET IN YOUR ROOM!"

I look out in the hall and see this kid, Marrow, drunk off his damn ass, key in his hand, and he can't get in the room! The master sergeant was yelling, "HEY YOU! GET IN YOUR DAMN ROOM!"

And every time he yelled, the kid would jump up in the air an' shit!

He finally got his drunk asshole in there, and found out that his room was the place that everybody goes when they're fucked up—the damn toilet. He fell asleep hangin' on underneath the toilet. That was the first night.

The next day I was talkin' to some girls, sayin', "Yeah, we're gonna leave here in a little while, maybe a couple of hours."

They said, "What you talkin' about?"

"Well," I told 'em, "they said that the first night we get here the boat wasn't gonna go nowhere, but it's gonna leave this mornin'." This is what I'd been told.

So they burst my bubble when they said, "We ain't goin' nowhere."

I said, "What you talkin' about?"

They said, "We're just gonna stay here in port for the next three nights."

I said, "WHAT!?!"

I'd been there a whole night before I found out. If I'd known that shit, I wouldn't have even come on the trip.

But we all had a real good time out there.

Welcome to Wolfburger!

That's what they teach ya in 94 Bravo school—the most effective way to strike at flies, making sure they don't fall on the floor and get wasted!

Spec. Karl Buehler, cook
348th Medical Detachment

The big problem with the Love Boat was the limited number of troops it could service. However, this wasn't a problem with another diversion, the "Wolfmobile," which was dreamed up by Army CW-4 Wesley Wolf, food service advisor for the theater.

The idea, as Chief Wolf envisioned it, was to get a hamburger and a coke into the hands of every serviceman in the field. This way, according to SFC Albert Ward, "they got 'Class A' rations without eating from the 'Roach Coaches'—the dirty, little wagons that sit beside the speedway and serve food, but charge a price for it."

SFC Ward, who helped operate the Host Nations Warehouse in Dharan, told me that 160 Wolfmobiles had been ordered, with about 60 already in service by late March. The Wolfmobiles and the food they served were donated to our troops by the Saudi government. All our military had to do was staff them.

The Wolfmobiles looked like little mobile homes without wheels, converted to contain a few grills and a couple of deep fryers. CW4 Thomas Butcher, who also worked with the Host Nations Warehouse, explained to me how they operated:

They're hamburger/hot dog stands. You can't pull 'em all around. Some of 'em are permanent, located on skids. Once you set 'em there with a forklift, then they're there.

But they've got the equipment in them to do hamburgers and hot dogs and french fries. Some of 'em can do grilled cheese sandwiches. They've also got a refrigerator and a freezer. You can cook chili if you want chili dogs or boil a little water for sanitation.

It normally takes about four cooks per shift to really get the production that you want. One of them little Wolfmobiles can put out a thousand meals an hour!

Installed from Kuwait City down to Dharan, the Wolfmobiles lined the main avenue for the redeployment of forces. Once in operation they often resembled little highway rest areas, a welcome sight to the field-weary travellers who hadn't seen a hamburger in months. A real morale builder.

But the Wolfmobiles had a couple of problems:

Our biggest problem with them is service, getting 'em repaired. The Saudis have two terms that we ran across a whole lot. One of 'em is *mafi mashkalla*, which means, "No problem!" Regardless of how big or how little it is, there's always "no problem," even if they can't do it! No problem, they'll try.

And the other one is a little word called *bokra*. And *bokra* is "tomorrow." It's always, "No problem, I'll take care of it tomorrow!"

Except tomorrow don't never get here! You end up having to nail 'em down to a day, a time, and an hour. "No 'bokra!' Tuesday! What time Tuesday? Ten o'clock Tuesday!"

And of course they show up around eleven or twelve o'clock. And because of the Ramadan religious holiday, they gotta quit at one o'clock.

On Friday, you wake up all bright and early. The service man was gonna be here at ten o'clock.

Ten o'clock comes and nothin' happens.

Eleven-thirty, nothing.

Twelve o'clock...then it dawns on you. Today's Friday. Friday's a religious day. Nobody works on Friday. That joker didn't intend to come to start with!

The other problem with the Wolfmobiles was the staffing. Army cooks, officially known as "94 Bravos," were needed to operate them. If you were a 94 Bravo, this could be an even bigger worry than getting repairs.

Spec. Karl Buehler, a 94 Bravo from the "Mickey Mouse Club," filled me in on why staffing was such a major concern. He said it all started about 10 years ago when the Army began phasing out its cooks, replacing them with civilian contractors in the mess halls across the United States and in its posts overseas. This reduced costs for the Army and seemed to work pretty well in the short run.

"The only thing is," said Buehler, "they got caught short when they found us in the middle of a war again. Our civilian contractors, of course, weren't gonna pick up their stuff and follow us into a combat zone. And now we're suffering for it."

Buehler went on to explain that King Fahd tried to compensate by supplying civilian contractors in Saudi to cook the meals at the consolidated mess facilities in large camps:

> That was all fine and dandy, until the war started and we had to move. When troops started to move out of the mess areas into the field, they needed 94 Bs to follow them and cook for them. And, of course, that's where we ran short.
> We now have these mobile kitchens called Wolfmobiles. They're real convenient, but with all these facilities opening—and they were never in the game plan—they needed to be staffed. So they started thinning us out quickly, through all the different companies. They just come, take the cooks, and sign 'em to a Wolfmobile.

"Nine times out of ten," added SFC Ward, "if the general says, 'You will load the Wolfmobiles up,' they're gonna get the personnel from somewhere! Ten times out of ten! They're gonna get 'em if they have to run 'em themselves."

So, what was it like to *work* in a Wolfmobile in Saudi Arabia? I just happened to meet SSgt. Carmen Donis, a cook fresh back from Wolfmobile assignment. As I sat listening, she and Specialist Buehler got on a runner, poking fun at "Wolfmobile reality" in a way Chief Wolf probably never would have appreciated. Still, it was all in good 94 Bravo fun:

> BUEHLER: How to get a job on a Wolfmobile in the Dharan theater? You have to have an MOS of 94B—or anywhere in the vicinity—be able to swat more than twenty flies a minute, and not have a good hiding place.
> You can see all the E-7s and E-8s from all the battalions walking around the mess halls, searching for cooks. And you can see the cooks in the mess halls scrambling into different corners, hiding. Because it's the *"Wolfburger patrol."*
> They're looking for cooks, or "volunteers," to go work 24-hour day shifts, 7 days a week, up in the fucking desert with no showers, in a place that has two or three inches of grease on the floor. They'll prepare the food, they'll serve it, and they'll clean up the feeding area—make that, the *grazing* area.
> Thousands of GIs come back from the war, and haven't even seen a hamburger for a couple of months, and they get "flyburgers."

> DONIS: What you wanna know about the Wolfburger? I'll tell you about the Wolfburger! It's about a million flies

flying all over the place. You sit on the highway, about three hours from Kuwait, and everybody that comes from up north, Iraq, that's the first burger they get before they get to the city. So you see all the guys that've been up there for seven months.

BUEHLER: Sergeant Donis, female-type E-6, enjoyed thoroughly greeting the thousands of sex-starved GIs on the highway back to civilization. One of the first females they encountered, she greeted them with a juicy flyburger.

DONIS: Those flies would be all over the burgers, man. And those guys, they didn't give a shit. They just said, *"Ahh, I'll eat it like that! I ain't seen a hamburger for seven months since I've been here!"* They just ate it.

BUEHLER: It was free.

DONIS: I asked a lot of them, "What if we were selling these hamburgers and hotdogs to you, and you had to pay two dollars for a hamburger?"
They said, "We wouldn't eat!"
The only reason they'd stop was because they were free. If they had to buy it, they wouldn't have stopped.
It was very unsanitary. Especially in the desert. We didn't have a screen or nothin'. There was dust all over the hotdogs and hamburgers. But they didn't close it down. All they believed in was givin' you your goddamned burger.

BUEHLER: Yes, Chief Wolf, that was a statement by E-6 Sergeant Donis, and she'd like to congratulate you on an operation well put together!
I can see a picture of a Wolfmobile sittin' in the middle of the desert, and three lines, about a mile long each, with a black cloud. And the black cloud is a swarm of flies, over the whole thing.
And each guy standing in line has a flyswatter in his hand, saying, "I can't wait to get my Wolfburger!"
They got a KP about fifty feet away, saying, "The Wolfburger you get for free, but you gotta buy your own flyswatter to get near the thing!"
And I see, next to the Wolfmobile, a full, unopened case of flypaper!

DONIS: Two weeks on the Wolfmobile was long enough for me. There's been people who worked it for three months.

BUEHLER: They're growing wings!

Those flies would be all over the burgers, man.
And those guys, they didn't give a shit.

At this point, Pilot Jim Korgis, from the 348th Medical Detachment, joined in the fun:

> *KORGIS:* Free condiments. You just open the burger bun and one lands.

> *DONIS:* It wasn't just Americans. There were British soldiers and people from Egypt. They'd be out there *all* the time!

> *BUEHLER:* Raving about the American food!

> *KORGIS:* They didn't really specify *beef* in the contract. There was a whole shipment had to be turned back because it was kangaroo meat.

> *BUEHLER:* But when it says "all beef," they're not lying

to you. From head to tail, from hoof to horn. I am not shittin' you!

KORGIS: In every burger I've ever had, there's something in there that just about cracked my tooth. The inspector has to work for the American Dental Association, I'm a firm believer in that.

BUEHLER: Watch out Mickey D's and Burger King! You can see it on the strip when you get back home. You're driving down the highway and you see the golden arches, and you damn sure know that, not more than two blocks down the road, you're gonna see a crown. Now, what are you gonna see in the middle of 'em?
A big fucking fly on a post! A wolf hunched over and a big ol' fly comin' down on him! You can see a picture of the burger bun, with a leaf of lettuce and three legs comin' out the side and a wing, and the head of the fly coming out one end. Welcome to Wolfburger! It's a high-protein burger. A lot of protein.

That's Entertainment?

They think we're crazy, but we have a lot of fun!

TSgt. Charles Walden
706th TFS Cajuns

In spite of all the joking about their shortcomings, the Love Boat and the Wolfmobile were enormously successful. The troops loved these diversions.

There were other officially sanctioned attempts to relieve troop stress and boredom. At Fleet Hospital 15, for instance, the Morale and Recreation Committee came up with the idea of theme nights— "Come As Your Favorite Cowboy Night," "M*A*S*H Look-alike Night," and "Aerobics from Hell Night," to name just a few.

These weren't just dress-up events. They also included variety shows, introducing local talents who would impersonate Rodney Dangerfield, wail on a harmonica, or sing gospel numbers.

Of course, there were movie nights all over the theater, though in the Gulf this usually meant a big color TV and a VCR, with anything from lawn chairs to stretcher crates for seats.

In addition to the officially orchestrated diversions, there were also plenty of the unofficial variety, which were equally appreciated. One extremely popular pastime was Nintendo Gameboy. This was also the big social event of the day in some areas, where people sat for hours watching other people play. Gameboys were everywhere in the Gulf. Pretty appropriate, I suppose, that one of the big diversions in Desert Storm would be as high-tech as the war itself.

HML-767 Maj. Thomas Cavanaugh, a veteran of another, lower-tech, war, was genuinely enthusiastic about the use of Gameboys. "All those Gameboys were a good thing for the troops," he told me.

"My boss asked me the other day, since we didn't have that in Vietnam, what did we have for diversion? I told him that back then we didn't need Gameboys. We had booze and whores everywhere we went!"

Another diversion was the golf. Practically every installation I visited had its own links. Fleet Hospital 15 had one, and, though it

*When I get home, I'm gonna be able to use
my sand wedge a lot better.*

was a mere four-hole course in a roadside drainage ditch, it did include such standard accoutrements as flags for each "green" and water traps with real water.

Over at Al Jubail Airport's Tent City, they had their own version of a Pro-Am driving range. This wasn't a simple facility to accommodate, either, given their cramped space. But somehow the marines worked it out—with minimal casualties. Only rarely did someone get struck by a golf ball as it sailed between the two lines of canvas billets. However, Maj. Jimbo Waites of the Nomads did capture one such feat with his camera, when Maj. Dick Coulter drove his ball into the head of a passing grunt.

Apparently, Coulter hollered at the guy, *"I said, 'FORE!'"*

To which the marine replied, "I was ready for SCUDs, but I wasn't ready for *golf balls!"*

Even some of the more desolate outposts provided for golfing. When I talked with WO-1 Joe Lassen, a pilot for the "Mickey Mouse

Club," he'd just returned from a mission in Kuwait, with his bag of clubs still hanging off his shoulder. Lassen, who carried his clubs along wherever he went, explained how the game was played up north:

> What we do is spend a week up there at the crossroads. We have two sand wedges and an eight iron. Once, one of our holes was a tank revetment, about a hundred and sixty yards—a par 4. We've also had to hit shithouses, shower buildings, and trash pits—anything, really.
>
> This time we did it up right. We had water bottles for the men's and ladies' tees. Weren't many ladies to play, but we had it all set up. We had nine holes. It was a nice, par 3 course.
>
> Yeah, there's been some really good golf played there. When I get home, I'm gonna be able to use my sand wedge and my short irons a lot better than my driver and long woods—for sure.

Sometimes, however, the troop-inspired diversions took a turn for the bizarre. And what could be more bizarre than Mardi Gras in the Saudi Arabian desert?

When I visited with two New Orleans-based reserve outfits in the Gulf, I was curious to learn how they had survived without their annual Mardi Gras. Turns out they hadn't—hadn't done without it, that is. Both units, the HML-767 Nomads at Al Jubail and the 706th TFS Cajuns at King Fahd, held their own parades and festivities.

I couldn't think of two places on earth that were more worlds apart than Saudi Arabia and New Orleans, but the Nomads and the Cajuns were determined, in their own little ways, to close that gap. But as Nomad CO Col. Al Boudreaux explained, the idea wasn't that well received by the Saudis.

"Mardi Gras is really big back in Louisiana and New Orleans, you know," the colonel explained. "Well, the Nomads threw a Mardi Gras parade here in Saudi. But on his way back from Riyadh, I guess the Prince of Somethin' didn't quite understand what we were doing."

"The morality police called us in," said Major Cavanaugh. "They were trying to pass it off as religious-connected, but I'm not too sure."

I could see Cavanaugh's point. It's hard to imagine that a float with scantily clad Navy nurses on it could be interpreted as "religious," but, in Saudi, sometimes it was a long way from words to meaning.

When the 706th knew it was going to war, the squadron had had the decency to warn the Iraqis that it was on the way. Maj. Seth "Growth" Wilson, one of the A-10 pilots, recalled the message they'd sent to Iraq: "The Cajuns are comin', and they've been told Iraqis are good to eat—but that they're an endangered species, so there's a limit of three!"

But nobody bothered to warn the Saudis about anything. So it really shouldn't have come as a surprise when the Nomad parade was busted.

Some new units were just arriving in-country as the 767's parade streamed down the flight line. Those new troops must have figured the war was over because, everywhere around them, people were throwing flags in the air, partying, and having a great old time.

"Yeah, they were unloading those guys off that 747," said Major

Waites, "all grunts getting ready to go. Those guys had just gotten off an 18-hour ride. They had tremendous jet lag. And they were getting bussed immediately to the front. But they marched right alongside our float, and there we were raisin' hell, bras on over our khakis and whippin' our digs around!"

"Follow us to Kuwait!" the Nomads yelled.

According to Waites, the colonel in charge of the new group wasn't at all sure he liked what he saw. Then he got hit in the head with an orange.

Meanwhile, over at King Fahd, the Cajuns parade also got rolling. SSgt. Raymond Montet told me a little of what went into it:

> The "First and Last Krewe of SCUDs"—that's what we named it. Saudi will probably never see a Mardi Gras parade again.
>
> We had a few nurses out here, who got all dressed down.
>
> We were trying to get some of the airplanes decked out in crepe paper, but they didn't buy it. So we opted for some fire trucks.

TSgt. Charles Walden certainly was dressed down for the occasion, as he reported to the flight line that day:

> I got some Mardi Gras stuff from New Orleans. When we were doing combat turns, getting the aircraft ready for another mission, I put on bikini underwear over my fatigues that said, "Happy Mardi Gras!" on the crotch. I had a big ol' purple, green and gold bow tie, and a Mardi Gras hat!
>
> The pilots got a kick out of it. "Chief," they said, "you're crazy! You must be from New Orleans!"

Briefly Speaking

Sure as the earth turns, the military never leaves anything to chance. There's a mandatory briefing for everything and anything that *could* happen, *is* happening, or *has* happened.

Lists were also drafted for the returnees to distribute to friends and loved ones.

Naturally, then, before heading home from the Gulf, our servicemen and women were briefed and rebriefed on what to expect when they returned stateside.

"When you get there, invite everybody to a big 'Welcome Home' party," suggested a Khobar Towers Army briefer, "or they'll come crawling up to you one at a time for years asking what it was like!"

Some units were thoughtful enough to provide their troops with handouts, listing tips for the big transition ahead:

MEMORANDUM STO-5000-01-23B

MAKING YOURSELF AT HOME AT HOME

1) Move into the smallest room in the house, establishing a six-by-three foot area of personal space.
2) Rip up the carpet, tear up the floor, and fill the joists with sand or cement.
3) Haul in all the scrap wood you can find and transform it into furniture.
4) Sandbag the room, four bags high, two deep. If you need more sandbags, steal them from your neighbors.
5) Replace all doors with tent flaps.
6) Don't water lawn, let it die to simulate desert environment.
7) Name your house, then post suggestive or insulting signs on it.

Corresponding lists were also drafted for the returnees to distribute to friends and loved ones at home:

MEMORANDUM STO-5000-02-48X

COMBATING POST-ARABIC STRESS DISORDER IN THE HOME ENVIRONMENT

1) Please make arrangements with all neighbors within 200 yards for my use of their bathrooms in the middle of the night.
2) Don't worry if I use the bathroom 6 or 7 times an hour, or stay in there for 30 to 40 minutes at a time—nothing's wrong, really.
3) When I take a shower, wait 2 minutes, then shut off the water in the basement, the hot water first.
4) Try to tolerate my sudden urges to go to the beach and roll around in the sand—I'm hooked on it.
5) Please spread a layer of sand all over the

house, particularly beside the bed and between the sheets.

6) Bear with me if I undress in the dark with a flashlight, shining it in your face as I fiddle with things.

7) Don't think it unusual if I invite all my bar buddies over to spend the night--I may suffer insomnia without a lot of farting and snoring people around me.

8) If I still can't sleep, please play the recording I made of a diesel generator at full volume.

9) On laundry day, expect me to cram my clothes in a plastic bag and mark it with the last four digits of my Social Security number.

10) Please ask the mailman to hold all my mail and deliver it en masse every four weeks--but tell him to pick up outgoing mail daily and process it "Free."

11) At meal time, don't mind if I either sit on the floor or stand up outside to eat.

12) Shoot a pigeon and have the cat eat it. Then shoot the cat and cook it. Serve it with rice or potatoes and insist that it's chicken.

13) Forgive me if I use at least one profane word in every *fucking* sentence.

Kiss My CB Ass

There's been sort of a rivalry between us Seabees and the Navy medical personnel since we've been here. We had to distinguish ourselves from them, so we separated the camp into "The Bees," and "The Trees"—referring to their "leafy," jungle-green camo gear.

CM-2 Carl Clark
Seabee, Fleet Hospital 15

The most difficult part of the entire deployment for many troops was watching others redeploy, as they continued to mark time. In honor of all those who waited while others went, I offer the following.

When I met with the Seabees, I figured I'd finally managed to catch up. After weeks of hearing stories about things that happened well before I arrived, here, at last, was an incident that had taken place just a few hours earlier.

Now, put yourself in the boots of one of those "Bees." Your motto is "We build. We fight. We party." You built Fleet Hospital 15 from scratch into the finest facility of its kind in the world. You fought the tedium and terror of confinement, month after interminable month, to keep the place operational. You partied when and where you could, but not *nearly* enough, especially compared to the medical staff—your generously perked brothers- and sisters-in-camp, who took all of the liberties in Bahrain, which you could only dream about.

And today, while you begin preparing for the arduous task of dismantling the joint, the "Trees" are leaving. What would you do to mark the occasion? Likely, what the "seven dwarfs" (the female Bees) did. You'd give the Trees a big going away—one they'd *never* forget.

EO-3 Letitia "Dopey" Risner recalled it for me:

Last night we were all sitting around. It was Millie's birthday, and as we sat there, we started conniving and conspiring—"We oughta do something really major, since they've been *so nice* to us!"

I don't know exactly whose idea it was, but we decided we'd moon their busses as they left.

But that wasn't good enough. We had to put our own little farewell message on our tushes.

247

So this morning, right after muster, we all took off and slid into one of the hootches, dropped our drawers and painted each other's asses! Everybody got a letter about five inches tall on each cheek.

According to another dwarf, CE-3 Casey "Grumpy" Carney, the Bees "found out which way the busses were headed, went over to the right road, and just waited for them to come by."

"We mooned ten busses," said Risner. *"Five hundred people!"*

"They loved it!" added Carney. "They were all waving, cheering and takin' pictures!"

And what was the farewell that they painted on their butts? CE-1 Steven Kulp revealed it all in a cartoon idea he gave me to immortalize the "Bun-flashing Bees":

Outgoing

A couple of weeks ago, the photocopier serviceman made a call at my studio in Red Lodge, Montana. While tuning up my machine, he glanced around at the Gulf War memorabilia I have hanging from the walls and asked if I had been over there.

"Sure was," I told him, explaining quickly that I had only been there as a cartoonist, not as a troop. Then my storyboard caught his eye, its 256 miniature book pages mounted in rows on the east wall like so many hunting trophies—my little victories, each representing a cartoon I'd drawn or a story I'd written for *This Ain't Hell....*

"You're writing a book on it?" he asked.

"That's right," I said.

"Good," he grinned. "Then I can find out what it was *really* like!"

Apparently this young man was a Marine reservist who, like thousands of other reserve troops, was activated for Desert Storm but never left the States. In fact, he'd arrived for special training at Camp Pendleton, California, the very day the war ended. So, instead of fighting Saddam, he was deployed temporarily along the Mexican border as a part of the federal drug interdiction program. According to him, all he'd gained from the whole experience was a healthy appetite for details on the war.

I thought about what the copier guy had said for quite a while after he'd gone. After all, in just a few words, he had restated my purpose for writing this book—to give the folks at home a candid, often humorous view of "what it was really like."

I'd like to think I've accomplished that mission in *This Ain't Hell...,* yet here I sit, knee-deep in scads of material that didn't make the final cut—not because it was less quality stuff, but because it demanded more space or time than I had available to do it justice.

Mafi mashkalla. I've reconciled this dilemma by committing myself to a second volume on the war.

My sincere thanks to all those who made this first volume possible, including: the troops—God bless them—who shared their wonderful stories and hospitality; the PAOs, who consistently pointed me in the right direction; the newspapers and senators who arranged for my travel orders; my publisher, Colonel Bob Kane, U.S. Army (retired), who gambled *big* on this crazy cartoonist's concept, and to Joan Griffin, his editing rep, who nursed it to fruition; Mark DeBauge, my friend in Denver, who found Presidio Press; Ken Mann at Carolina 92FM in Nags Head, who inspired the interviewing process; Glenn Eure, my Gulf travelling buddy, who provided constant encouragement and laughs; and, finally, my dear son Colin, who employed his perseverance, good humor, vision, and many skills in bringing his old man's book to print.

See ya,

Barry